Mutual Aid, Everyday Anarchy

Mutual Aid, Everyday Anarchy

Essays on Colin Ward

Edited by Andrew Kelly

Five Leaves Publications
www.fiveleaves.co.uk

Mutual Aid, Everyday Anarchy:
Essays on Colin Ward
Edited by Andrew Kelly

Published in 2024 by Five Leaves Publications

14a Long Row, Swann's Yard, Nottingham NG1 2DH

www.fiveleaves.co.uk

www.fiveleavesbookshop.co.uk

ISBN 978-1-915434-22-7

Printed in Great Britain

In memory of Colin and Harriet

Contents

Introduction: Why Colin Ward Remains Important
Andrew Kelly 9

01. Colin Ward: The Life and Times of an Ordinary
Anarchist
Sophie Scott-Brown 13

02. A Memorable Day: When Meeting a Hero Works
Out Well
Tessa Coombes 19

03. Principled, Generous and Kind: How Colin Ward
Influenced Me
Sheila Rowbotham 23

04. Colin Ward and Me (and my Mum)
Ted Fowler 29

05. Take Ten: Paid Educational Leave and the Art of
Citizenship
Catherine Burke 35

06. A Different Kind of Planning: Learning from
Colin Ward
Rob Cowan 41

07. A Seed Beneath the Snow: Everyday Anarchism
Paul Dobraszczyk 47

08. Vandalism, Ownership and Play in the City
Luca Csepely-Knorr and Amber Roberts 53

09. The Child in the City
Alice Ferguson 59

10. Colin Ward: Visions of Autonomy
   Gillian Darley   67

11. Colin Ward: A Quiet Voice of Dissent
   Ruth Kinna   73

12. Arcadia Everywhere
   David Knight   77

13. Anarchism as Theory of Organisation
   Martin Parker   81

14. Resonating with Colin Ward
   Sol Pérez-Martínez   89

15. Play, Education, Creativity and Activism: The
   Legacies of Colin Ward
   Martin Stott   95

16. Colin Ward and the Sound of Anarchy
   Stuart White   101

17. 'A marginal person like me'?
   Patrick Wright   107

18. Schools Without Walls
   Ken Worpole   113

19. Reworking 'the relations between people and their
   environment': Colin Ward's Quietly Radical Urbanism
   Dan Hill   121

20. Anarchism's Good Ancestor
   Roman Krznaric   129

The Contributors   137

Acknowledgements   143

Further Reading   145

Introduction

Why Colin Ward Remains Important

Andrew Kelly

I never met Colin Ward, but I feel he has been with me for 40 years. I first read Colin in *New Society*. This led me to search for his articles and then his books. Later, as I developed projects and festivals on future cities, I turned to his work repeatedly for advice on transport, housing, sustainable places, new towns, organising community activity. If I did a book on those who have influenced me – much like Colin's wonderful book on the people who influenced him – he would be on my list.

For more than three decades I ran cultural projects for Bristol Ideas. Realising that 2024 was the centenary of Colin's birth I thought this was an opportunity to look in detail at his life and his work. I called together a small group of people who had known him. This group grew larger – and more and more enthusiastic – as the word spread and many project ideas were discussed. The end of Bristol Ideas in April 2024 meant that we could make progress with little, though we were able to bring this book together, and many of the ideas discussed will happen at some point, run by others.

This collection of new essays, written by those influenced by him and his work, shows the profound impact he has had. Essays cover first encounters and the many years of friendship that followed; ideas of mutual aid, everyday anarchy, creative dissent and scepticism; the right to places and cities; the influence Colin had on people as parents and environmental thinkers; Colin as a colleague and as an editor, in the Town and Country Planning Association and the *Bulletin of Environmental Education*; the journey towards utopia and what can be achieved along the way; his work on allotments, holiday camps and new ways of organising; and Colin as a good ancestor.

Our writers cover his generosity, optimism and open-mindedness; the trust he had in people and the interest he took in their work; his constant learning, reading and writing; his belief in the importance of involving people affected by the changes they were facing, not just in that overused term consultation, but in actively seeking out ideas from people and communities. They tell stories of the time he devoted to them and the bags of books he gave them. They write of his ideas and the way they have applied these.

I wish that we had involved Colin in our projects in Bristol – what a difference he would have made to them – though I like to think he has been a guiding spirit along the way. I wish too that we could have done more in 2024, though this is tempered by an awareness, mentioned by some in our group, that Colin would not have wanted a centennial celebration; the application of his ideas would instead provide a lasting legacy.

2024 marked the end of 14 years of Conservative domination of the economy and politics. The new government is still developing policy and legislation. There is talk of extended devolution, more social housing, a green transition, better public transport, and even some new towns. Ministers would do well to look at what Colin Ward wrote on these and other issues to help guide them to help create change that lasts.

Modest he may have been, but this gentle anarchist has much to offer today and tomorrow when creating new and better places for all. He was a fine writer who ranged widely. A writer and thinker we can all continue to read and use in our everyday life and work.

01. Colin Ward

The Life and Times of an Ordinary Anarchist

Sophie Scott-Brown

Colin Ward stood for an intimate anarchism that pulsed through all aspects of life. To him, there was no firm line between the private and the public. As a self-identified propagandist rather than thinker, his priority was to revitalise anarchism in the popular imagination by stressing how its principles of self-reliance, cooperation and mutual aid were already part of our daily life in our homes, communities, schools and workplaces.

He considered a similar rebranding necessary for the figure of the anarchist. Out went the dark, brooding action-hero – like Mikhail Bakunin – or the brilliant, bespectacled intellectual – like Pyotr Kropotkin – and in came anyone whose most remarkable feature was just how unremarkable they were. 'Anyone' was literally any one of us struggling to get by while keeping a few principles intact and not losing our heads completely. This sensible character did not gaze into the middle-distance, imagining federations of intentional communities all around the world. They looked about themselves in the imperfect present for all the liberty they could scrape and squeeze from their current situations.

As every good anarchist propagandist knows, you cannot tell people how to be anarchists, you can only show them the possibilities and hope they will feel inspired. In part, Ward did this through his elegant ethnographies of mutual aid in action such as *Arcadia for All: The Legacy of a Makeshift Landscape* (1984) and *Goodnight Campers!: The History of the British Holiday Camp* (1986) with *Dennis Hardy, or The Allotment: Its Landscape and Culture* (1988) with David Crouch. But if Ward was anything, he was a columnist and a virtuoso one at that. The self-contained, episodic character of a column allowed him to show anarchism reinventing itself in a range of different scenarios, like a kind of picaresque novel. Meanwhile, the personal quality of the stories helped emphasise the 'ordinariness' of anarchist principles.

Over the years, Ward often used himself, family and friends as a model for the 'Anyone Anarchist', not that he formally approved of autobiography. On being asked to write his life story, Ward replied, in the magazine *Resurgence*: 'I have read plenty of such books and have seen how the first few chapters are the most absorbing, after which they tend to trail off into a catalogue of names, jobs and encounters. This in itself is a depressing thought. How can it be that for many people everything after childhood is an anti-climax. And I'm mindful too of Orwell's sharp comment that an autobiography that is not a history of failures is a pack of lies.'

As someone planning to write Ward's life story, I wondered how to address this tension between the autobiographical style of his writing and the equally strong antipathy to autobiography. Did that mean that the Ward who appeared in those cosy yarns was really 'a pack of lies', a clever propaganda ploy to make us believe anarchism was perfectly normal? Reflecting on his life in radical journalism, he seemed to admit as much in a 1991 interview with Tony Gibson: 'you could say it was a confidence trick, by making the reader believe that anarchism was not a way-out notion, but was an aspect of everyday life, one of the currents of contemporary thought, and therefore had to be taken seriously'.

In the end, I decided it was futile to try and tease a 'real' Ward from a 'presented' one. After all, being an anarchist propagandist was an important part of his life. Crafting the 'Anyone Anarchist' as an alter-ego to perform his ideas for him was all part of that. Moreover, reading his homely anecdotes closely could tell me a lot about why 'Anyone' was so important to his political ideals.

Early examples were tantalisingly brief but showed a natural talent for free association. In 'Out and About', a short-lived series in *Freedom* (1950-1951), an aunt's daily train commute demonstrated why railways should be run by rail workers, while his abortive efforts to paint his house in Ellerby Street revealed the trouble with trying to regulate the building industry and its supply chains. Later, in his longer 'Comment' column (1952-1956), an account of a late summer's gleaning potatoes took in the politics of the humble spud from its use in maintaining Incan imperialism to its role in suppressing the Irish poor *before* the famine (making potatoes the dietary staple for the Irish peasantry kept them fed cheaply and stopped them aspiring to the higher wages necessary for buying wheat).

It was Ward's 'Comment: On the Human Scale' (*Freedom*, 27 August 1955) where he really found his style. It told the bright and cheery tale of a weekend at the village fete where he competed with the other men in the vegetable show – 'my gooseberries were too early, my raspberries too late, my peas too thin, my beans too short, my celery too green and my surviving carrot too solitary' – while the ladies 'openly reckoned their chances in the baking and home crafts tent'. All in all, 'the sun shone, the sports were hilarious, an old lady won a pig in the draw and wondered what to do with it, gardening techniques were discussed, prize-winners were proud and the rest of us resolved to do better next year.'

Suddenly, the tone chilled, 'the show is one of the only occasions in the year when the village acts like a community and not the scattered collection of weekend farmers, retired majors, rural proletarian, petty gentry, small shopkeepers, struggling smallholders and commuting stockbrokers that it largely is.' Real community, he continued, was created by living and working together, something centralised planning and capitalism had combined to destroy. The popularity of the fete showed people's longing for something no longer available to them.

Unbeknown to the younger Ward, 'On the Human Scale' rehearsed the 'rural writing' style he would use in 'Fringe Benefits' (*New Statesman and Society*) 30 years later. Here again, he transformed apparently trivial events from village life into miniature anarchist parables. For example, there was the story of John, a neighbour presented with a broken pianola (15 December 1989). Eager to restore the instrument to its former glory, John sought the advice of three wise men, an aeronautical engineer, a civil engineer and a chemist, all of whom scratched their heads, made a few wild suggestions, but, for all their expertise, could not solve the problem. John, unburdened by professional knowledge, was forced to improvise a solution which turned out to work perfectly well.

Elsewhere, there was Nobby Clark, an ex-Navy man and former occupant of Ward's Suffolk cottage. Despite having little money, Nobby was adept at making do, going so far as to hand paint grain patterns on plain wood to mimic expensive floorboards. 'Miss H' and 'Miss C' moved in after Nobby had died. Living almost entirely outside of the 'formal economy', the two women lived tough lives, growing most of their own food. For all their hard work, they still made time to maintain a glorious rose garden ('Fringe Benefits', *New Statesman and Society*, 23 and 30 August 1991).

It was not just his choice of subject matter that he put to work for the cause, it was his writing style, too. Each tiny story was perfectly constructed with an easy, even pace. His narrative voice was gentle, conversational rather than hectoring, shot through with flashes of peppery humour over some outrageous breach of common sense or other. Notably, despite the personal nature of the material, he maintained an air of distance, sharing his readers' outside view, exchanging metaphorical winks with them at the foolishness of the world. By the same token, all his anarchist solutions – decentralisation, dispersal, worker and dweller control, schools without walls and community education – were quietly repackaged as practical good sense rather than as romance or idealism.

As Ward's biographer, I compared the columns with other autobiographical sources such as *Talking Anarchy* (2003), his rich and absorbing interview with David Goodway. Here again, all was not as it seemed. The project was conducted entirely by written correspondence during which Ward carefully composed his answers, adding and cutting questions as he went along. All Goodway's efforts to probe or provoke were firmly rebuffed. Picking up on a reference to friction between the anarchist factions, he asked Ward, 'that's an interesting remark! Who stayed aloof?' The reply was cool and dismissive, 'I think it's inevitable rather than interesting.' Subject closed.

Presenting himself as an 'ordinary' person—rather than a quarrelsome radical—was key to restoring anarchism to the mainstream but there was, I realised, another more fundamental reason for this amiable reserve. As WH Auden had it, in a line Ward was fond of quoting, 'Private faces in public places, Are wiser and nicer, Than public faces in private places' (*Orators*, 1932). In other words, Ward believed that true liberty began with self-possession, in keeping some small piece of yourself back as an anchor in the chaos of modern life.

02. A Memorable Day

When Meeting a Hero
Works Out Well

Tessa Coombes

Meeting someone whose work you have read and admired for some time is always an amazing thing to do, but when you are a young, inexperienced researcher and that person is a well-respected author and writer – well, it's quite daunting. That's how I felt when I met Colin Ward.

I first read some of Colin's work when I was an A-Level student in the early 1980s. As a response to the political system under Thatcher I was going through an anarchist phase, with punk rock music (Crass and Dead Kennedys featuring strongly) and anarchist reading in the era of anarcho-punk. I read some work by anarchists like George Woodcock and William Godwin, as well as the more traditional writers like Pierre-Joseph Proudhon, Mikhail Bakunin and Pyotr Kropotkin. They resonated with me, with my anger at what was happening around me, with my ideals of equality and fairness. Colin's work first came to my attention when I delved into housing and anarchism as part of a geography assignment I was doing at the time. *Housing: An Anarchist Approach* (1976) and *Arcadia for All: The Legacy of a Makeshift Landscape* (written with Dennis Hardy in 1984) were the first books of Colin's that I read and I have revisited them many times since. The principles of self-help, self-organised communities and direct action when considering housing issues and problems seemed attractive to me then, and now.

As a town planning student at University of the West of England I returned to Colin's work. In our second year (1985-1986) we did a course on the philosophy of planning and were given the option of doing one of the set essays or choosing a question of our own. I decided to do an essay on anarchism and planning and covered more of Colin's work on housing, land ownership and direct action in his books such as *Anarchy in Action* (1973), *Utopia* (1974), *Tenants Take Over* (1974) and *The Child in the City* (1978).

I also joined the Town and Country Planning Association (TCPA) soon after I graduated as a town planner in 1988. I was a fan of the Garden City movement and the work of Ebenezer Howard as the basis for planning and design, compared to the dull and uninspiring private sector-led approach to planning in the 1980s and 1990s. Colin wrote a regular column for the TCPA for many years, so I kept in touch with his writing related to planning and housing through reading the TCPA journal.

I returned to UWE as a research assistant a year after I graduated, and I spent seven years there doing research and teaching. It was my teaching that led me to get in touch with Colin. I was teaching housing and planning, comparative planning and the theory of planning to different year groups. As part of this teaching we were encouraged to bring in outside speakers to widen the experience our students received.

I remember trying to think of people who might make an impact on the students and give them something different to think about. My shortlist of all the usual suspects left me uninspired. I then thought about some of the reading I had been doing as part of some research I was conducting at the time on Thatcherism and planning, and kept coming back to Colin's work. Without a great deal of hope, an email was sent to Colin asking if he'd be interested in travelling to Bristol to give a guest lecture and a staff seminar. I honestly didn't think I'd hear back, as I assumed he was busy and wouldn't necessarily have time to bother with such a request from someone he didn't know. Several other academics on different topics had ignored me.

Imagine my surprise when I did get a response, and a positive one at that. We quickly made arrangements for him to visit and for me to collect him from the train station. I stood there on the platform at Bristol Parkway, with a vague idea of what he looked like from the back cover of one of his books, waiting for his train to arrive. I remember being quite nervous – this was someone whose books I had read avidly for years and admired greatly. My first impression on greeting Colin was of a gentle, kindly person with a sharp and inquisitive mind. He looked like a grandfatherly figure to me – me in my mid-20s and him in his mid-to-late-60s – but once we started talking he was engaging, interesting and asked searching questions about my research and what I was doing.

Needless to say, Colin's talk went down a storm with the students and the staff seminar was one of the best I ever went to. His lecture was centred on town planning, with nods towards anarchist philosophy, but very much focused on practical applications of self-help communities like the post-war squatters' movement, the Diggers and Plotlanders. He discussed land ownership and how the planning system reinforced the link between land ownership and wealth. Speaking to the students afterwards, I remember the energy and enthusiasm they had for some of the ideas Colin had discussed. The staff seminar went on beyond the hour and a half allocated as people had lots of questions. I can remember getting nervous that he would miss his train, so had to call it to a close while the discussion was still ongoing.

Meeting Colin was a real treat (it isn't always the case with heroes). My lasting impression was of a gentle, unassuming man who seemed to shy away from the limelight and who even seemed bemused by people seeking his views. Having said that, he also came across as a strong character, unafraid to give his views and very willing to be challenged, relishing those challenges and keen to debate with others. His inquiring mind and quiet intelligence were something most of us can only aspire to.

From the moment I met Colin at the station to the moment we waved him off again, it's a day I will never forget. Indeed, even though it was over 30 years ago, I can still clearly remember the meeting, the discussion and how it felt, and this was in the early 1990s, before social media and the ability to share pictures and comments more widely. I wish I had photos to remember the day, but I do at least have my personal memories of meeting one of my all-time academic heroes.

03. Principled, Generous and Kind

How Colin Ward Influenced Me

Sheila Rowbotham

I can see Colin Ward in my mind's eye slightly stooped, exuding warmth, amiability and an inner resolve. But it was his attentiveness to others and his capacity to listen with a remarkable kind of encouraging intensity which struck me most of all.

I knew Colin's name long before I met him in person. When I became a student at Oxford in the early 1960s, I gravitated towards small clusters of Marxist socialists. My mediaeval history tutor wisely advised me to 'Read Marx, not people on Marx', so I did, struggling but invigorated. However, as I went on to read more widely about the history of the left, a biography of the anarchist Emma Goldman really excited me. Here was a woman who defied conventions, hung out with hobos and campaigned for birth control.

Emma Goldman led me to Colin's magazine *Anarchy*, on sale in Oxford bookshops, and through it I discovered a radical politics of daily living and relating that tallied with my own experiences and observation. *Anarchy* challenged hierarchies which had intimidated me in families, schools, sexual relationships, the state. Best of all, it showed that you could *do* something about these.

'Doing' was in the air in the early 1960s. The Campaign for Nuclear Disarmament (CND) marches, from Aldermaston to London, pitted protesters against military and police power and this was accentuated when the Committee of 100 started to take non-violent direct action. My close friend from school, Barbara Raines, was carried off by the police for sitting down. I joined a breakaway of several hundred people from the CND march which headed to a Regional Seat of Government (RSG), designed to preserve an elite if an atom bomb dropped. After that, teenagers in local CND groups roamed through woods around the country, on the lookout for yet more RSGs. We direct actionists constituted a broad alliance. When the artist Richard Wallace was arrested on a charge of obstruction for selling *Peace News* in Oxford, socialists and anarchists defended him.

So, by chance, I was radicalised at a time when there was interaction between socialist and anarchist ideas in Britain as well as in other countries. This mixing continued, although the context changed in the late 1960s after the May events in France. Then, when women's liberation groups started to form in Britain and elsewhere, we took ideas of direct action and control beyond the workplace, into daily life and personal relationships.

Women's Liberation alerted me to the history of women's activism, and I became interested in the socialist feminist Dora Russell, who had been advocating women's sexual freedom since the 1920s and was also an inveterate peace campaigner. When we met, I discovered that she also happened to be the mother-in-law of Colin Ward. By that time, I had come across him through the magazine *New Society*. Open-ended, with a radical edge, *New Society* brought together contributors with a wide range of views, documenting everyday life in Britain and airing dissenting ideas on social policy reforms. Moreover, it extended into a critique of urban planning and state secrecy.

Colin's emphasis on listening carefully to what people said about their immediate surroundings enabled him to look critically at both right and left versions of planning from on top. He took this approach into his educational work in the Town and Country Planning Association. Despite its solemn sounding name, the Association's inspiration had been the Victorian utopian Ebenezer Howard, who had promoted the concept of garden cities. Ideas of cooperation and the anarchist Kropotkin's 'mutual aid' had inspired early twentieth century thinking about living in communities. Colin added his insistence on grounding utopias in what people themselves wanted.

Perhaps this may sound obvious, but this was not an automatic starting point at this time for many professional architects, regardless of their politics. I remember being taken by an architect friend to see a much-lauded example of Sheffield brutalism and immediately noticing with scepticism how women with shopping and prams would have to push up the elongated passageways, zig-zagging outside the building to reach their homes.

Upon becoming a mother in 1977 in Hackney, London, I learned by myself just how difficult it was to move around on public transport with a baby and a pushchair. Colin's book, *The Child in the City* (1978), became ever more relevant as my son grew older and I read it again and again. It elaborated the approach I had imbibed from *Anarchy*, of beginning with the incongruities of how we actually lived. It was such a simple yet revolutionary proposition, to imagine a city designed to meet the needs of children of all ages, instead of accommodating cars.

In the early 1980s I started working at the Greater London Council (GLC). Through the Industry and Employment Committee, the left councillors had decided to develop an alternative economic policy in opposition to the devastation being wrought by Margaret Thatcher's government. I was in the Popular Planning Unit (PPU) which encouraged Londoners to express their needs, wants and desires and worked with them on ways to meet these.

In November 1985, tenants from the Divis Flats in Northern Ireland arrived in London for an exhibition of photographs mounted by the Town and Country Planning Association which visually demonstrated the flats' barracks-like design and detailed just how grim they were to live in. Colin, who had taken up their cause, gently but assiduously shepherded us around.

Interest in what the GLC was doing had spread beyond London and, after visiting various GLC housing projects, the tenants from Divis came to meet the leader of the council, Ken Livingstone, in the Popular Planning office. Deciding they would be hungry after tramping around, I had gone shopping for food. We all munched away as Ken spoke. The Divis tenants were particularly impressed by the activism of residents at Coin Street, which had resulted in revitalised co-operative housing, including shops, a market and small businesses with the backing of the GLC. They were also interested in the 'People's Plan' for the Royal Docks. Tenants and trade unionists in opposition to powerful financial interests sought ideas from a wide range of docklands groups and, helped by members of the PPU, put these together in a large, widely distributed pamphlet with colourful photographs.

I do not know what Colin thought about what we were doing. Historically, after all, municipal socialism had been part of the state bureaucracy. In the 1980s, the GLC's tentacles extended into the London boroughs, overseeing the journey of solid waste down the Thames and regulating the myriad traffic lights of a city with a population of a small country. On the other hand, Colin was interested in how small units could relate to large ones. In a few short years, the left Labour councillors at the GLC had brought into being a series of small groups like the PPU within the metropolitan administrative structure which operated through participatory democracy and connected with many Londoners directly.

Moreover, we Popular Planners quickly learned how schemes we might devise would never come to lasting fruition without agitation and association among people outside the GLC. I felt lucky to be able to observe how the combination of pressure from groups of Londoners and the possibility of public resources, contrived to extend what could be achieved in myriad ways.

With a remit to serve the welfare of Londoners, like alternative moles we diligently burrowed away supporting community projects, while stinging like fleas by publicising what the Conservative government's policies were doing to people's lives. Our efforts proved sufficiently undermining and irritating to Margaret Thatcher for her to abolish us in 1986.

Shortly after the abolition of the GLC, Dora Russell died and her daughter, Harriet Ward, asked me to speak at the memorial. Listening to Harriet's wry description of her childhood made me question my idealisation of a bohemian upbringing, so utterly unlike my own. When her perceptive memoir of her father, Griffin Barry, *A Man of Small Importance*, was published many years later in 2003, it enabled me to understand how stimulating but puzzling Harriet's early life must have been. At the end, she thanks 'Colin Ward, my resident encyclopaedia for support and assistance beyond enumeration'.

Many, including myself, who did not know Colin so well, would echo these thanks to a probing thinker and committed doer who expressed complex ideas when he wrote with a careful clarity. I remember him as a principled but generous spirit who sought common ground and was prepared to accept people like myself, who did not share all his views, with great kindness.

04. Colin Ward and Me (and my Mum)

Ted Fowler

During the second half of my life, I learnt the name and have increasingly understood the relevance and powerful influence of Colin Ward the writer. Before then I was (unwittingly) influenced by his work. Talking about Colin recently helped me crystalise the emotions as well as the analyses that have informed my political, civic and socially entrepreneurial life.

As a youngster in Falmouth in the early 1970s, I skived off school, but I enjoyed going to the library and learning for myself: there was always a geographer and a historian drawing maps of how industry would link up with sources of power and settlements, transport routes. Falmouth was great for that. I also knew that there was something vital missing – for instance there wasn't much about practical learning and errors and there wasn't much about people except the 'great and the good'. It all felt a bit like talking tactics without scoring goals.

My mother was basic staff at a home for what was then called 'The Mentally Subnormal'. She was also curious and engaged. My dad, an optician, was a great contributor to the town. In those days we believed in progress and contemporary design and technology – new towns, roads, modern homes. Yet there were also weird, interesting people not succumbing to the dominant streamlined metaphors. These played out for instance in my mother's Women's Liberation Group, the wonderful music, and squatting communities and *New Society* which I read avidly in the library. We discussed a lot.

I was pushed out of school so I went to Camborne Tech. Emboldened by pamphlets (big ideas, small enough to digest) we set about starting a student union and wrote a launch magazine. The magazine got banned – my article about gay liberation wasn't considered acceptable for a college. Eventually a 'printer poet' Dennis Gould published it although I'd gone by then. The key issue here for me was the dissonance between the neat world of what was acceptable in society (common sense), and the untidy, struggling, and brave world of people.

I left home and took up travelling and seasonal work in Europe and the UK, mixing it up with some study, mostly by myself. My core trade was as a lambing shepherd, which I learned from kind people on the job, fishing and dock work and other such manual, semi-skilled trades.

My mother – a Dutch woman who knew things could be done differently – also left our home at the age of 48, and, having been encouraged by Jennie Lee's Open University, took a course in Town and Country Planning at Middlesex Polytechnic. She loved it and, although she didn't have the confidence to take the finals, she got (and gave) a huge amount of encouragement and support from what I believe was a young faculty.

One common friend I had with Mum was Dot Davies, also at Middlesex. Dot took me around South East England taking photos for Colin Ward of post-war informal communities she called plotlands. We talked about the subjects of her photos, and about people making sense of their lives and the world. My mother and myself were both learning to contribute in our different ways. I realised that the combination of seven years travelling for work and studying alone was leading me away from any kind of community life. Mum built on her learning and provided home, practical skills and intellectual grist for a wide range of people.

There was a kind of politics within this, which I felt was worth exploring if I wanted to play my part in the wider social world. With Colin Ward I found someone whose work was honestly and effectively engaged with the awkward and the not so neat world of people. He took people seriously; no nostalgia, no avoiding the very real conflicts, but with a fascination in how people cope and also in how authority managed (or didn't manage) the challenges, when the plotlands were established and long term as well.

By then I'd arrived in Bristol, working as a stone-wall builder. Slowly but surely conversations within my community helped me develop a much-needed framework and ideas for practical work. For me, Colin also encouraged respect for, and engagement with, people with different lives, ideas and useful experience: a learning network that burgeoned, and has nothing to do with status, within and beyond the organs of organised labour and civic society.

I became both an Avon County Councillor for St. Pauls and a playworker and support worker for isolated older and young people. After this I was a Postie and lived in the heart of that community. Colin Ward's *The Child in the City* made sense to me.

It was a call to empathy and action, to respect children, recognise the world they live in, encourage their creativity and their sociability to mitigate the harms of civilisation. I realised that being child-friendly is also being people-friendly.

I was enthused by people who had so much to offer in community as well as professional contexts. My role was more than decision making, it was about robust understandings – to interpret each to each. Sometimes we could initiate streams of work that respected the needs of all, but especially to open up space for better outcomes: my constituents, as in other working-class areas, wanted so much more from life than simply equal opportunities.

Also vital was the pamphlet Colin wrote with Ruth Rendell, *Undermining the Central Line.* Here I found a distillation of my increasing frustration that Westminster really didn't want local people to make choices of substance, as well as the lack of accountability for the general absence of vision. They argued 'The British political system has given our current rulers the absolute right to sell off services into the private market…but you will have to agree (reader) that it is the fault of all of us, and our parents, in taking for granted that central government knows best.'

Far too much of public discourse on local place making fails to recognise complexity and interdependence among practitioners at all levels. We have lost local authority over much that is important in our everyday lives. Councils seem to be more accountable to government for funding and regulation than to place and voters, being in explicit competition with each other for patronage. These undermine our ambitions, our role as stewards, and those vital skills we develop by working together through our own problems.

Twenty or so years ago there was a brief flurry of initiatives, sponsored by government, yet informed by the movement that Colin Ward was part of. These regional Centres of Excellence engaged with councillors, planners, community activists, architects, public health, all involved in place-making. A broader range of skills were recognised and encouraged through the 2004 Egan Review on Skills for Sustainable Communities. There was leadership and empowerment to achieve this including charging councils with developing sustainable communities across the range of built environment, health, transport, cultural and economic activities.

In Bristol (despite government) we have established more recently Bristol and Bath Regional Capital (BBRC) as an investor for public benefit, and with an intention to be a store of local capital, encouraging local talent and creativity. Due to government policies BBRC has to be outside democratic control, so guerilla activities like this are fast emerging. There are also powerful possibilities in the world of green and blue infrastructure in which I am mostly now active. These citizens-led initiatives are usually good in themselves, but they are small in capacity, often undercapitalised so often short-term and hard work, especially due to the global competitive environment in which they strive.

Few senior policy makers recognise the current drift of real power away from people, perhaps largely because they don't have Colin's robust appreciation of more widely distributed personal agency and history. The role for civil society as a home for challenge and innovation, is potentially even greater nowadays, but the place, fit and permissive platform that a political, rather than technocratic, council can provide for local action is now weak.

Back to my Mum. She moved back to the Netherlands in the 1980s, to a small independently minded town in Zeeland – she took pride in what they were achieving and often referred me to her Enfield schooling and the everyday heroes of local place-making. Now I can see other people challenging the degradation of our public realm, digging into politics and developing place-shaping crafts, building on Colin Ward's game-changing contributions.

05. Take Ten

Paid Educational Leave and the Art of Citizenship

Catherine Burke

One of my favourite books by Colin Ward is *Influences: Voices of Creative Dissent* (1991). In this book, Ward takes delight in introducing the reader to the words and actions of individuals he had most admired and learned from. These included characters who, through their writing and actions, recognised the power of education to change the individual and the collective: William Godwin (1756-1836), Mary Wollstonecraft (1759-1797), Patrick Geddes (1854-1932) and Paul Goodman (1911-1972). Influence takes many forms. For Ward, these 'quiet voices of dissent and scepticism' – mostly neglected by the academy and generally hidden from view – spoke directly of alternative ways of living and learning. In turn, Ward's own words and quiet anarchism came to indirectly influence my experience of working in 1980s' Sheffield on an adult education project called Take Ten.

Over the past 40 years, state support for adult education, especially informal learning, has greatly diminished. However, when Take Ten was launched during the early 1980s, there was still, in Sheffield at least, a commitment by the Local Education Authority to resource and encourage community development through informal education rooted in local neighbourhoods. Take Ten Paid Educational Leave (1983-1993) was a major initiative of Sheffield City Council. It offered low paid manual and clerical council workers the chance to reconnect with education on ten days over ten consecutive weeks without loss of pay. These were typically waste operatives, cleaners, home helps and residential home carers. They also included school cooks, construction workers and administrative officers who looked after the city's infrastructure and public services. Employees who had left school with few, if any, qualifications were particularly encouraged to apply for 'time off to learn'.

With the coming to power in 1979 of the first Thatcher Conservative government, the then-leadership of the city council were aware that, as a radical Labour authority, their values and capacities would inevitably come under attack. It was considered critically important to develop resilience and solidarity among the workforce, highlighting the mutual interests of manual and non-manual workers. Understanding how the city worked required learning the 'art and technique of citizenship'. With the support of the relevant trade unions, Take Ten was intended to become an important means towards achieving this objective.

A team of four experienced adult educators, including myself, were appointed, given a budget, and allowed considerable freedom to shape the pedagogy. The only requirements were that we promote confidence in re-engaging with education and develop an enhanced understanding of the politics of the city. Participants should learn about decision-making processes, how they could take part and how power was exercised by the local and national state. One of the team, Graham Birkin, brought to the project his recent experience as a community worker at Centerprise in Hackney. There he had witnessed a strong commitment to egalitarian working practices as well as the power of literacy and publication projects supported by photography. As the nominal team leader of Take Ten, in a typical gesture of solidarity and mutual respect, Graham rejected the implied hierarchy of his role and, for the duration of the project, informally shared the difference in his salary among other members of the team.

Ward understood the power and political potential of education when experienced as meaningful and 'grounded … in respect for the learner' of whatever age. At the heart of the Take Ten curriculum was the nurturing of a deep respect for the everyday work experience of those recruited to the programme. Throughout, formally and informally, the team modelled a way of working that demonstrated a commitment to anti-racism, anti-sexism and collective values.

In his writing about education, Ward had, like many others in the 1970s, proposed practical ways of building a curriculum by means of a radical change in power relations between learner and teacher, and between school and community. In *The Child in the City* (1978), Ward described an array of possibilities that might be achieved by recognising the city as a rich educational resource. He suggested that doing so offered increasing levels of agency – 'learning *through* the city, learning *about* the city, learning to *use* the city, to *control* the city or to *change* the city'. On reflection, I can see how these possibilities were evident in the ways that we came to use the city as a resource in shaping the Take Ten experience. We might have gone further with time, but at least we managed to learn to use the city and sketch out further possibilities.

To build the curriculum, once a degree of trust was established, Take Ten participants were encouraged to identify, in dialogue with their peers, their own concerns and questions, often reflecting the local, national or international news of the time. Over ten years, no ten-week cohort was the same. Our task as 'educators' was to identify how best to help them address the issues identified and to meet their learning needs. Often this took us out of the 'classroom' and into the city to meet with experts of all kinds. Thirty council workers divided into three groups, each shepherded by one of the team – a street pedagogue. Sometimes we took the opportunity to visit other cities: Liverpool, to find out about the history of slavery and local housing initiatives; Manchester, to meet with campaigners striving to stop a hospital closure. In London, a group that was keen to know more about how the media worked visited the BBC to meet the producer of *Newsnight*, while another group visited the Greater London Council in session. These could be described in Ward's words as 'journeys of exploration' or 'street seminars'. It was only much later in my career that I came across Ward and Anthony Fyson's book *Streetwork: The Exploding School* (1973), which described, with children and young people in mind, the kind of enquiry-based learning that had been a fundamental aspect of the Take Ten experience.

Ward illuminated the idea of the city as a resource for learning through his many articles published in the *Bulletin of*

Environmental Education (*BEE*, 1971-1989). Several cover images of the *BEE* show children using cameras in support of their urban explorations and investigations. Although the *BEE* was aimed at secondary school communities, the same processes and tools for learning proved to be useful in the Take Ten context. At the start of each ten-week course, participants were issued with a loaded camera and were asked to take images that would assist in explaining to each other the nature of their work and working conditions. These photographs were used to promote discussion and to trigger writing. In turn, writing developed confidence and furthered curiosity about self and others.

As noted at the start of this essay, influence takes many forms, and as well as Ward there were many influences shaping the Take Ten project: the work of Paulo Freire, John Holt, Ivan Illich and the 'revolution in the English primary school' of the 1960s, for example. So, what of the outcomes?

Participation in this unusual collective experience of learning, rooted in a mutually determined curriculum, led some to seek out further opportunities to study. Many enrolled on access courses that offered a route into higher education. Others became more active in their trade unions, some becoming shop stewards. Some formed women's groups, joined or set up tenants' groups. Others got the writing bug: a collection of writing about work by course members was published in 1985. Many simply enjoyed relief from their work responsibilities for ten days without loss of pay.

The Take Ten project came to an end in the early 1990s as the financial cost became too great and more formal accredited adult learning increasingly began to attract resources. The team members went on to take up further opportunities to provide political education in various fields. I eventually moved into the higher education sector, finishing my career as Professor of the History of Education at the University of Cambridge. At Cambridge, I often found myself reflecting on the Take Ten years as being formative for me as a teacher and scholar. From those years, I carried with me knowledge that an alternative progressive experience of education for teachers and learners was possible. This partly explains how I came to research and write about the history of such past adventures in education. This was due in no small measure to my coming to know and practice a kind of pedagogy that I hope Colin Ward would have recognised and admired.

06. A Different Kind of Planning

Learning from Colin Ward

Rob Cowan

I have in my head a number of voices who talk to me as I am writing and editing. A couple of them are sub-editors with whom I once worked, who guide me on their favourite points of punctuation or sentence construction. And for many years there was Colin Ward. He often popped up in my interior monologue to say something along the lines of: 'Yes, what you are about to write is the accepted wisdom but is it really true?' Annoyingly, I would then have to think again.

Colin seemed to be in the top of my head. In reality, in the late 1970s and early 1980s he was actually at the top of my head. We both worked at the Town and Country Planning Association (TCPA), him promoting environmental education and me providing planning aid to community groups. My desk was in a large room in John Nash's splendid Carlton House Terrace, and Colin's was immediately above it on a mezzanine floor that had more recently been inserted. From Colin's desk to mine ran a massive steel ladder, to be used if ever Colin's papers caught fire and he and his colleagues in the Education Unit needed an alternative means of escape. There never was a fire, and what drifted down from the mezzanine were nuggets of Colin's wisdom and the copy for his regular column for the TCPA journal, *Town and Country Planning*, which I edited.

Editing Colin's articles took no time at all. It was more or less a matter of marking up his neatly typed pages for the printer. I sometimes thought that he quoted other writers too much: reading a rather long extract, I often used to think, 'Colin could have expressed that so much better if he had used his own words'. He sometimes may have quoted as a way of filling the space with minimum effort, but generally it was because he was looking to draw out the essential anarchism from the most unlikely of sources. He would quote from a Conservative politician, for example, with whom one might have thought that he had nothing in common, because he had detected in the politician's dislike of mindless authority a common interest in giving people the freedom to run their own lives.

Colin corrected people who supposed that anarchy was the opposite of organisation. Anarchy, I often heard him say, meant the absence of government and the absence of authority. Could there be social organisation without authority, without government? As an anarchist, Colin claimed that there could be and that it was desirable that there should be. As he put it, the fact there was no route map to utopia did not mean that there were no routes to more accessible destinations. His life's work was to trace those routes and find ways of making them more accessible.

Finding himself working in an organisation devoted to town and country planning, Colin highlighted the potential strengths and weaknesses of the planners' role. He spoke of the 'bureaucratic managerialism' that he identified as the consequence of an alliance between Fabians and radical conservatives at the end of the nineteenth century. This, he said, had led to the takeover of socialism by the bureaucratic managers responsible for the worst types of town planning, unsuccessful council housing and collectivism. His vision was of a type of planning, free of domination by professionals, that enabled people to create places and housing for themselves.

He pointed to the 'theory of loose parts'. The theory states that the degree of inventiveness and creativity, and the possibility of discovery in an environment, are directly proportional to the number and kind of variables in it. The painter, sculptor and educator Simon Nicholson (son of artists Ben Nicholson and Barbara Hepworth), formulating the theory in the 1970s, argued that the imposed environment (the one in which the citizen has only a passive part to play) resulted from cultural elitism. Colin explained that the missing cultural element was the aesthetic of a variable, manipulable, malleable environment: the aesthetic of loose parts. The missing political element was the politics of participation, of user control and of self-managing, self-regulating communities. He described such a community in his 1975 proposal for a 'do-it-yourself new town'. The TCPA further developed that idea in 1979 with its (unachieved) prospectus for a 'third garden city', aimed at bringing Ebenezer Howard's garden city concept up to date.

There was no shortage of practical examples of resourceful people getting things done for Colin to point to, such as the self-build housing pioneer and architect Walter Segal. The problems that self-builders experienced were not to do with the process of building itself. Rather, they were the result of the inflated price of land, the rigidities of planning and building controls, and the difficulty of getting mortgage loans for anything out of the ordinary. They were all made worse by the assumption of both regulatory authorities and providers of finance, that a house should be a fully finished product right from the start, rather than a simple basic structure that could grow over time as needs changed, and as labour and income could be spared. Segal's achievement, Colin told us, was to devise a way of simplifying the process of building so that it could be undertaken by anyone, cheaply and quickly.

To conventional town planners, the plotland development that was common in South East England the few decades before 1939 was exactly what the planning system was meant to prevent. Areas of farmland were divided into small plots and sold as holiday homes or smallholdings, often without the usual infrastructure of paved roads, piped water and mains drainage. Colin, by contrast, was fascinated by the way in which a landscape composed of a gridiron of grassy tracks, sparsely filled with army huts, old railway coaches, sheds, shanties and chalets, slowly evolved into ordinary suburban development, created by its residents. He looked for a different kind of planning system, one that would give people the chance of continuously upgrading the place where they lived, making owner occupation or running a smallholding a reality for people who started with nothing more than a plot of unserviced land.

Such a planning system would need a different kind of

planning professional. Colin mused on the lesson of Sir Herbert Manzoni (1899-1972), city engineer of Birmingham in 1935-1969. Manzoni planned the 'concrete collar' of the inner ring road that so disastrously carved up the centre of the city in the 1960s. 'I'm not interested in small solutions, only big ones,' Manzoni said. On another occasion, Manzoni announced: 'I have never been very certain as to the value of tangible links to the past. As to Birmingham's buildings, there is little of real worth in our architecture. Its replacement should be an improvement, provided we keep a few monuments as museum pieces to past ages'.

Colin pointed out that Manzoni was not an ignorant technocrat spiralling up the local authority promotion circuit. He was a cultivated and dedicated public servant devoted to his city and using the best wisdom of the period to solve its traffic problems. In retrospect, Colin said, we could cynically conclude that more fortunate cities had an engineer who was lazy, close to retirement or addicted to golf, as traffic would then have been managed through one-way systems, park-and-ride provision or neglect, and the physical fabric of the city would have remained intact.

What Colin valued was the variety that reflected the lives of the people of a place, as he evoked in his 1989 book *Welcome, Thinner City: Urban Survival in the 1990s*. In the past, he wrote, 'a city fancier knew without seeing that there must be a lorry-driver's snack bar round the next corner, as accurately as any predecessor centuries earlier would locate a coaching inn. A poor traveller would know where he could find cheap lodgings and the prospect of casual work. An itinerant salesman would know that a shop on that particular site would not pick up enough trade to be safe for credit. A lecher knew, without any red lights, where the red-light district was. Drinkers knew where to find their particular kind of bar. Criminologists could take one look at a place and predict the patterns of offences. Wholesalers and hucksters, junk men and junkies, model aeroplane enthusiasts and people selling leotards to dancing academies all developed a city sense which is a guide to the specialised functions for which cities originally arose.' Colin complained: 'The buildings of the rebuilt city do not talk any more, at least not in a language that makes sense to the citizen'.

When Colin came across someone whose opinions he really could not stomach, he would sometimes say: 'Come the revolution, he'll be put up against the wall and shot.' We did not need telling that this was a joke, highlighting the lazy stereotype of an anarchist as a violent revolutionary. It was all the more of a joke because Colin was the most gentle and generous of people, to whom his typewriter and his brilliant lectures were all the weapons he would ever need.

07. A Seed Beneath the Snow

Everyday Anarchism

Paul Dobraszczyk

Colin Ward consistently argued that anarchism was always present in society, rather than a utopia to be realised in the future: 'an anarchist society, a society which organises itself without authority, is always in existence, like a seed beneath the snow'. This is an idea of anarchism – and of politics more generally – that has resonated with many others, particularly those seeking to develop a more inclusive and generous kind of politics than partisan ideologies. The late David Graeber has been perhaps the most vocal in this respect: his polemical essay 'Are You An Anarchist? The Answer May Surprise You!' is an anarchist version of a religious tract. It takes examples of everyday behaviours, whether negotiating other people on a crowded bus or working as a volunteer, and turns them into a passionate argument for anarchism as a universal, if mostly unacknowledged, way of simply being in the world. Geographer Simon Springer (*The Anarchist Roots of Geography: Towards Spatial Emancipation*, 2016) has reiterated this emphasis on everyday anarchism, inviting us to see signs of an emancipatory politics in the most prosaic acts of generosity: 'every time you have ever invited friends over to dinner, jaywalked, mowed your neighbour's lawn, skipped a day at work, looked after your brother's kids, questioned your professor, borrowed your mother-in-law's car, disregarded a posted sign, or returned a favour, you have – perhaps unknowingly – engaged in anarchist principles'.

Springer calls this kind of human behaviour a 'prefigurative politics' (a term originally coined by Carl Boggs), meaning that it is revolutionary in a very different way from conventional understandings of that word, particularly in Marxist readings. Here, in the present moment, certain kinds of behaviour literally enact the politics of anarchism, often without their protagonists even knowing it. This is perhaps a secular variation of Jesus' exhortation of unselfconscious virtue: 'do not let your left hand know what your right hand is doing, so that your giving may be in secret' (Matthew 6:4). Ward framed his own interest in prefigurative anarchism – whether seen in the actions of allotment holders, squatters or children in playgrounds, to cite but a few examples of his rich field of studies – as fundamental to broadening the appeal of this kind of politics beyond a narrow group of activists. He wanted to win people over to anarchist ideas 'precisely through drawing upon the common experience of the informal, transient, self-organising networks of relationships that in fact make the human community possible'. In this respect, Ward and those he has influenced point us back to the root of the meanings of politics itself: the Greek word *politeia* describing how citizens in the *polis* organised urban life. Of course, in antiquity, urban citizenship was an exclusive affair (women and enslaved people had no part in this kind of politics); but the Greek definition of politics nevertheless holds open the possibility of a fully participatory organisation of everyday life, if citizenship can indeed be extended to everyone.

I find the generosity of Ward's vision of anarchist politics compelling, but it comes with its own set of problems. First, can it be said that there is any such thing as an unconscious form of politics? Surely, putting the label 'anarchist' on kinds of behaviour that are not acknowledged as such runs the risk of misinterpretation, even solipsism: the belief that what others do is there to merely confirm your own understanding of the world? In drawing attention to everyday behaviour, what Ward, Graeber and Springer argue for is a recognition that there is already a consensus out there as to what people generally recognise as valuable in their lives: namely, freedom, generosity and respect towards others. Some may not hold to these values, but the assumption is that the overwhelming majority of people do. Asserting the near universality of certain values is a powerful way of expanding politics beyond the partisan dogmas that so often characterise political parties of all persuasions. It has the effect of opening up the very meaning of politics to a much wider remit that centres on values rather than policies, on meaning rather than structure. Here, I would argue that the associated risks are far less than the potential benefits, which are no less than a transformation of political life from the roots upwards.

A second criticism of prefigurative politics is that it can only ever operate at a very small scale. There is a world of difference between an impromptu dinner party and the business of government, especially of large-scale institutions and infrastructure which always transcend individuals. Political theorist David Harvey has been particularly vocal in his criticism of anarchism as a politics of the local that can never realistically negotiate the exceptional complexity which characterises contemporary cities and their governance. In *Rebel Cities: From the Right to the City to the Urban Revolution* (2013), Harvey argues that hierarchical forms of governance are always required at larger scales – he cites the mitigation of climate change as an example – because questions of what is held in common are always contested. The more people that are involved in decision-making, the more complex these questions become, consensus becoming ever more unlikely. For Harvey, the solution is a 'nested' hierarchy of governance that becomes more established as the scale of the issues to be addressed increases. The problem with this argument, as Springer makes clear, is that even thinking about scale results in a moving away from lived experience – it's a tool that allows questions of consensus to be side-lined because its very purpose is to distract from those questions. Scale quite literally 'sets things apart' – it is an abstraction of lived reality. Quoting the dictum often attributed to Mahatma Gandhi, 'be the change you want to see in the world', Springer argues that scale is a 'theoretical distraction, a drawing away from the grounded particularities of the everyday'.

In this reading, it is simply not possible to map the future, to know where individual actions will lead: this is an illusion of control. It is therefore an affront to impose political dogmas on any one individual's behaviour. This may seem wildly impractical, even downright irresponsible, but that is because anarchism stems from a radical uprooting of established notions of politics. Almost all of our ideas about politics involve notions of exclusion, whether this is acknowledged or not. To even assert a particular political affiliation is to exclude others, let alone to belong to a political party. It's clear that any organised politics needs to balance the need to belong with that of individual autonomy. Anarchism – conceived as a prefigurative politics – asks if it might be possible for us to remain open to difference in the face of the often forceful desire to exclude. In my view, this 'remaining open' constitutes the primary political force of anarchism; it is abandoned only when absolutely necessary and, then, only with regret in the hope that any exclusion can be reversed.

The question of what might be constructed out of such a personal politics is an apposite one to conclude this short reflection. In scientific studies of the buildings made by social insects – beehives, ants' and wasps' nests and termite mounds – it has been demonstrated that complex structures can emerge from very simple behaviours of individual insects (in this case, animals without brains or even neural networks). The reason is that it only takes a small number of rules to produce a higher level of order – what is known as emergence in behavioural studies. Now I am not suggesting for a moment that humans are like insects; rather that complex organisation need not be dependent on the implementation of hierarchical systems of governance. Perhaps the 'simple' values of anarchism – mutualism, self-organisation, autonomy – can operate in a similar way to pheromones in insects – they are the rules that govern behaviours and which, if held fast to and in numbers, can produce the structures that always seem so out of reach. Perhaps the maxim that your left hand should not know what your right hand is doing is not an exemplar of Christian piety, but rather the basis on which a new political and social order might emerge.

08. Vandalism, Ownership and Play in the City

Luca Csepely-Knorr and Amber Roberts

An article in June 2023 in *The Guardian* ('UK families tell of threats and police warnings over children playing in street') discussed the need for, and difficulties of, finding spaces for children and young people to play, highlighting the continued debate regarding design and the role of open spaces in our social lives. Here, we discuss questions of ownership, children's play and anti-social behaviour through the writings and designs of Colin Ward and Michael Brown, who not only shared an interest in these questions, but who were also collaborating on bringing them to the attention of their contemporaries.

Throughout the early 1970s, vandalism and anti-social behaviour were becoming increasing problems in inner-city areas, along with growing dereliction and population decrease following the campaign for new towns and the associated movement of people from city centres. In particular, the cities of Liverpool and Glasgow became notorious and many disciplines joined the debate, from architects and planners to sociologists, housing managers and local authorities. Early on in this debate, Colin Ward edited the book *Vandalism* (1973) before *The Child in the City* (1978). The book brought together experts from a variety of disciplines to provide food for thought on different aspects of vandalism. The book was a timely response to the question that was quickly becoming a pressing issue. As Ward described in the introduction, '[t]hose who earn a living by modifying the environment have an interest in the durability of their handiwork, those charged with its maintenance are usually concerned with its survival, those who inhabit it are expected to show some degree of care for it. Consequently we all have opinions on vandalism'

A year before the publication of *Vandalism*, Ward edited an essay by landscape architect Michael Brown (1923-1996) on housing landscapes which shed light on issues discussed in his book from the point of view of 'those who earn a living by modifying the environment'. Ideas in Ward's book were realised in the projects of Michael Brown during the period in question.

Brown was an Edinburgh-born architect and landscape architect whose work combined leading Scottish and American spatial theories in mid-century Britain. His projects covered all scales of landscape architecture and are of special interest due to his commitment to integrating the theories and practices of both disciplines and countries, resulting in a body of work that was both inventive and realistic. Brown wrote in 'Placemaking – Start with Facts; Finish with Values' (*Landscape Architecture* 1981) that 'the art and aesthetic delight of landscape must emerge out of solving down-to-earth problems elegantly and simply' and, with this focus on the solution of 'down-to-earth problems', Brown's work navigated somewhat complex tensions of the profession that existed both then and now by advocating an objective, theoretical and interdisciplinary approach that can be seen in his work on design and vandalism in the 1970s.

Both Brown and Ward aimed to add nuance to the standard view of vandalism in that period which characterised it as a problem with 'senseless' working-class males. Instead, Brown argued that it was a social reaction to a lack of opportunities, a sense of ownership and creative expression in urban environments. Ward's editorial commentary aligns with this view. Indeed, in *Vandalism* Armstrong and Wilson argue in the case of Glasgow (the Easterhouse estate specifically) that 'much of what we call deviant behaviour is a convenient label for what is really social protest'. In *The Child in the City*, Ward quotes Iona and Peter Opie as they question 'are children, in some of their games, expressing something more than high spirits, something of which not even they, perhaps, are aware?... may it be some impulse of protest in the tribe?'

Brown's theoretical approach can be seen as the driving force for his housing landscapes at Livingstone Road, part of the Winstanley Road Estate in Battersea in London. Throughout the project, he explored the potential that courtyard layouts presented in creating defensible spaces to encourage a sense of ownership in residents. The open spaces of Livingstone Road were each given a distinct character through the careful detailing of landform on sunken and raised levels to create soft spaces embellished with sculptures and wall panels.

With this design decision he aimed to create solutions that, as he wrote in 1972, could 'draw on involvement, they need to share these motives, they need to give incentives to see what is possible and to show people, by a demonstration of living examples in their own community, what can be done... There is a need for diversification of ownerships and types of occupation.' Despite a restricted use of lawns, Brown proposed extensive street tree planting throughout the scheme, which resulted in green views afforded from every household. The courtyard typology served as a functional extension of the house by providing space to live out family life in the city, addressing a significant cultural issue of the period in the migration of young families to the new towns and suburbs due to the lack of appropriate services and spaces to support family life in city centres. As he argued in his 'Placemaking' essay: 'What is important – and this is true for all age groups – is that users, consumers, tenants and owners (and we are often one or more of these) are made to feel that the whole of their habitation belongs to them: Quite simply, for a design to be integrated with its users' needs, it must offer choices and possibilities. Our role is to make places that lend themselves to a multitude of uses.'

Brown also had a uniquely deep understanding of the ways children use space and of the importance of design for play and its role in the city, evident in the housing schemes he developed throughout his career. In the Livingstone Road project he created places that children can use creatively while playing. As he explained: 'Spaces are needed where play can be invented with simple things like cardboard boxes and string; for there need be little special equipment then to wear out, break down, become out of date or unfashionable'. This understanding, which treated children in the same way as the grown-up users, put Brown into the forefront of thinkers of new types of play spaces, and the idea recurred as one of the central questions of *The Child in the City*: 'How do we rear citizens who will make the city their own?'.

There is an implicit argument running through Brown's 1972 essay that touches on the idea of planners as vandals. It places responsibility for vandalism issues with planners and designers making ill-informed and somewhat destructive decisions. As he argues, 'I think we are far too little aware of the real physical and social consequences of what we are doing. The rising standards of our aspirations make us risk destroying the character of our towns'. Ward added further nuance to the argument by saying that 'once we adopt this standpoint we lose our stereotype of 'the vandal' and we may also become aware that his activities are far less devastating, lethal and expensive, than the destruction and attrition of the urban environment by other forces in society.'

The recent pandemic has proved the importance of open spaces around us and the lack of equity in our abilities to use them. The questions of the housing, climate and biodiversity crises all bring to the forefront the questions of quality open spaces. Brown and Ward's vision of the role of these spaces in society could not be more relevant. Brown argued that it 'poses a special challenge to us: to devise new ways of planning that will enable a changing emphasis of needs to be observed without laying waste and destroying existing assets that are man-made or natural, and indeed without destroying the resources of the land'. It is now time to reconsider how we can use their work and ideas for better spaces for tomorrow.

09. The Child in the City

Alice Ferguson

Growing up in Bristol, I was a child in the city at the exact time Colin Ward was writing *The Child in the City* (1978). Both at the time and with hindsight, I felt I had plenty of freedom to roam and to play out with my friends. Ward however, while warning against both a rose-tinted view of the past and a homogenous view of children quoting – Margaret Mead, he reminds us that 'The child doesn't exist. Only children exist' – , saw a general trajectory towards children's loss of freedom even then, pointing a finger towards capitalism and car-centric planning.

He was right, yet I was blissfully unaware of this seismic change happening around me. Although we kids were well aware of certain dangers and boundaries – we would avoid crossing the busy main road unaccompanied, for example – I certainly don't remember feeling hemmed in. My experience was filtered by family circumstances (middle-class) and, perhaps more importantly, by the neighbourhood we lived in: a formerly (and, in 2023, once again) 'posh' part of the city, re-colonised in the 1960s by bohemian ex-students starting families.

The community this created was not diverse, either socio-economically or ethnically, but it was full of politically engaged, free-thinking adults with a strong sense of collectivity and a DIY attitude to local change-making. It felt a safe and welcoming environment, something like the proverbial village it takes to raise a child. Front doors were generally open and we knew our friends' parents by their first names. An early and formative experience was our whole street coming together to resurface the road with reclaimed cobblestones one summer. The adults took time off work and the children 'helped' and played out. An outsized, anarchic anti-speed bump was created and the street became even more our space.

As children, we had the run of the neighbourhood. Aged about eight onwards, our patch extended past the school and down to the accidental, undesignated non-spaces – what planners call SLOAP ('space left over after planning') – under the 1960s-built flyovers bringing vast numbers of cars into the city. There we would hang out, roller-skate and organise skipping games with a huge rope and loads of kids of all ages and backgrounds. We were getting exercise and gaining social skills and life experience without anyone thinking about it.

One of the things I love about Ward's view of childhood is his resistance to any kind of romanticism or sanitisation: the beauty is in the real and the messy. In the first chapter of *The Child in the City*, 'Paradise Lost?', Ward discusses the myth making that adults do about the physical environments of their childhoods. He invites us to 'Go back to some unrevisited paradise and see how pathetically ordinary it actually is to your adult eye'. I did this, revisiting a place very near home that I had 'run away' to for an illicit picnic with an older girl who lived up the road. It was a sad piece of flat concrete overlooking a dual carriageway. But at the time it was a secret place: one I shouldn't have been in and where I wouldn't be found. That made it magical, both at the time and in my memory of it.

But while in our 'paradise', car-centric planning was already happening all around us, changing the fabric of our city and – though we weren't aware of it – in Ward's words, 'whittling away' both street life and our access to space.

I was only vaguely aware of my father's efforts to push back against this paradigm, first as a city planner fresh out of architectural school (and strongly influenced by Jane Jacobs), then as the city's youngest councillor from 1973-79. Sadly, neither he, Ward, nor any others sounding the alarm about the damage car-centric planning would do to the life of cities and to children's lives were listened to.

Fast-forward 30 years and I was a mother of two young children living just down the road – across the flyover – from my childhood stomping ground. Car ownership in the UK had more than doubled and streets were no longer the shared space I had grown up with. My daughter was turning eight, yet her relationship with the space around her could not have been more different to my own at the same age and this stark contrast was hitting me hard. As soon as we stepped outside the front door, traffic danger was ever-present. The speed, volume and general entitlement of cars meant I didn't feel comfortable letting her play out on our own street or call for a friend on the other side, let alone cross several roads to get to the park. Between 1978 and 2008, children's lives had changed even more than in the 30 years running up to Ward writing *The Child in the City*.

And it wasn't just the physical environment that had changed. There had also been a huge shift in attitude. Towards parents, children, streets and public space. Towards children being *in* space. It no longer felt normal or acceptable for children to be outside, unaccompanied, playing without purpose. Parents were meant to organise and supervise every moment of their lives. The result was a lot of time isolated and indoors for children – and a lot of stress for parents. This felt wrong to me.

I had already come across Mayer Hillman's research on children's independent mobility (started in the early 1970s and referenced by Ward) when working for Sustrans on their Safe Routes to Schools campaign between 2002-2004. As the mother of a toddler at that time, Hillman's thesis that children's freedom had been unthinkingly sacrificed to the car resonated strongly. A few years later, as my children grew and needed more autonomy, I felt I needed to try and do something to change things.

I had the good fortune of finding several parent allies, including Ingrid Skeels, who had set up a volunteer park group with the aim of restoring young people's sense of belonging in their local space. My neighbour, the artist and street performer Amy Rose, was also starting to think about children's loss of freedom to roam and imagining how our doorstep space could be reclaimed and repurposed. Together we discovered and discussed Jane Jacobs, Christopher Alexander and Colin Ward. Writing decades previously, these visionaries clearly saw what was happening and where we were heading. They articulated exactly what we were feeling and experiencing now: a world where children were not considered, where there was no room for them, where they had to be, in the words of Roger Hart, 'contained'. Fired-up by this, in the spirit of anarchism and inspired by David Engwicht, we began thinking of possible DIY ways to push back.

Amy and I came up with the idea of simply closing our street to through-traffic for a short time as a temporary way of reclaiming the space, making children visible and starting a conversation. We called this model 'playing out' and the idea began to get attention. Other local parents heard about it and wanted to do the same thing. A grassroots movement began so, with Ingrid and others, we set up Playing Out as a non-profit organisation to grow this campaign, support others to play out across the country, and call for wider policy and social change towards restoring children's freedom.

That was 12 years ago. Since then, more than 1,500 street and estate communities have 'played out' regularly in Bristol and many other cities including London, Leeds, Brighton, Newcastle, Manchester, Birmingham and Liverpool. Playing Out has become a respected voice for children's right to play outside where they live and continues to push for this to be a serious consideration across relevant policy areas, including planning, transport and housing.

We are not alone in this mission and many of our closest allies would also count *The Child in the City* as a touchstone.

Tim Gill, author of *Urban Playground: How Child-Friendly Planning and Design Can Save Cities* (2020), is a world leader in making the case for children's 'everyday freedoms' to be designed into neighbourhoods and the wider public realm. In his article 'What do child-friendly neighbourhoods look and feel like?', he quotes Ward's provocation that 'the failure of an urban environment can be measured in direct proportion to the number of playgrounds': the whole city should be available to children.

Dinah Bornat is a London-based architect whose work has become largely about persuading housing developers to better consider the needs of children. She came across Ward as a student and says, 'Ward is like Jane Jacobs in that he challenges us to look at the city and settlements and the ways in which people use them, in a radically different way to the mainstream'.

In fact, Ward's book can probably be largely credited with inspiring the entire international Child-Friendly City movement, which aims to place children at the heart of planning and wider decision-making.

I am writing this following a personal study tour of Belgium and the Netherlands, visiting child-friendly streets and spaces and meeting some of the campaigners and professionals who have been involved in creating them. Even those who had not consciously come across Ward shared much of his philosophy, as is clear in the essay 'Return of the child-friendly city? How social movements are changing European urban areas' in *The Conversation* (26 April 2023) by Jonne Silonsaari and Marco te Brömmelstroet of the University of Amsterdam which argues, 'children should not be reduced to mere "future investments" or "adults of tomorrow". They are also people with present day rights to citizenship, participation and autonomy in their living environments'.

I have come away feeling that Ward still has much to offer the world of urban planning and the world in general. In particular, the following guiding principles or considerations could completely change the way things are done, to create better environments for everyone:

- Children are people: individuals with rights, actors with agency
- Children interact with/in space differently from adults
- Spatial justice is key to a fairer, happier and healthier society
- DIY, collective action is an important means to changing the status quo and to resisting change.

Ward's superpower is that he gets all this across – and much more – in a writing style that is readable, poetic, detailed and personal. In particular, he manages to convincingly convey a child's experience of living in an adult-built environment. He showed 50 years ago what is even more true today: this child's-eye view is exactly what is needed in order to sort out the mess we adults have collectively created of our cities.

10. Colin Ward

Visions of Autonomy

Gillian Darley

In my youth I had the temerity to propose writing and photographing an overview of 'model' villages. Among the shoals of carefully designed estate cottages and decent quality industrial villages that made up most of the entries in the gazetteer at the end of the book, there were a number that had been built on different lines, tending towards the visionary, be that a version of communal endeavour or philanthropic idealism. From the start I was particularly drawn to these more utopian planning experiments. As Colin Ward puts it in *Influences: Voices of Creative Dissent* (1991), 'the fact that there is no route-map to utopia does not mean that there are no routes to more accessible destinations.'

Surprisingly, although I couldn't claim any postgraduate qualification nor had ever had anything published, my outline received a quick and positive response from the commissioning editor at the Architectural Press, Godfrey Golzen. Who was it who had given an independent opinion on my proposal, a book that I wanted to call *Villages of Vision*? I suspect I now have the answer.

Colin must have been a frequent visitor to Godfrey's office at Queen Anne's Gate, as they met to discuss a book which would recalibrate the links between city and child, ranging far beyond Britain's shores. *The Child in the City* (1978) was Golzen's inspired commission, perfectly fitting Colin's particular insights and drawing on his phenomenally wide reading. The editor's then-wife, Ann, was also the ideal candidate to be the photographer and, as Colin put it in his acknowledgements, 'instantly grasped what pictures were needed and went out and took them'. They were admirably unsentimental, with an immediacy and observational empathy that tuned with the author's attitude.

It would have been obvious enough for the publisher to ask his about-to-be author's advice on the feasibility of a title about planned and utopian villages. His proven interest in alternative housing, in the outcomes of self-determination, as seen in the aspirations of the Garden City movement, but more particularly in self-build and co-operative endeavours – topics he would expand on and tussle with over the coming decades – made him an ideal sounding-board for my proposal. Or so I speculate.

Although garden cities did not figure in my book, those turn-of-the-century villages which sprang from the same ground, and involved many of the same people did; New Earswick, Port Sunlight and Hampstead Garden Suburb in particular. Soon after its publication, I was invited to sit on the Executive Committee of the Town and Country Planning Association and it was there that I first encountered Colin, whose mid-life training as a teacher and previous experience in architectural offices, as well his voracious appetite for reading, made him an ideal choice to be the education officer at the Town and Country Planning Association and to edit their new *Bulletin of Environmental Education.*

I began to read Colin's work, which touched on so much of what interested me. Occasionally I received postcards and brief notes from him offering warm encouragement, thanking me for my positive (how could they be otherwise?) reviews and sometimes, especially as we became more regular correspondents, signposts to his own plans. After my biography of housing reformer Octavia Hill came out in 1990, he told me he was preparing 'a book of my lectures called *Talking Houses*... then I am going to do a Green Book called *Influences* about the people who influenced me. Self-indulgence has no limits.' A less self-indulgent man I have yet to meet.

As my own work zig-zagged between journalism, broadcasting and longer-term projects, I felt I had an arms' length mentor – along, I know, with many others working in similar fields. A rich combination of being an educator, social observer and an acute listener informed everything Colin touched, whether collaborative books or his own. The element that strikes me most forcibly now is the open-mindedness and clear moral compass that guided his approach, so tangible when he gently questioned people in Christopher Martin's deft BBC TV film, *New Town, Home Town* (1979). Rewatching it I am struck by how unerringly Colin identifies the key aspects in each dissimilar example (Harlow, Peterlee, Runcorn, Milton Keynes), mirroring the shifting priorities of the region in question, its economics, demographics, society and politics, past and present. He is informative, addressing a general audience, while giving us a surprisingly incisive report. His non-partisan analysis is shot through with principle, privileging the kind of 'creative dissent' which he regarded highly and practiced for himself. When Colin interviews residents, he allows their voices and views to emerge unvarnished. He is gently quizzical towards the young men who express a longing to be back in the city (be it London or Liverpool) or the more thoughtful young women (often living under the same roof) who have come to see the virtues of where they live. He poses questions, assesses outcomes, recognises difficulties but remains humane and disarmingly frank.

In the book which followed in 1993 under the same title, commissioned by the Gulbenkian Foundation, Colin quoted Lewis Mumford's words about Ebenezer Howard, 'his gift of sweet reasonableness'. They could well be applied to Colin himself, as an advocate of those nascent towns to a largely indifferent, if not negative, public. It came out just as the Commission for the New Towns replaced the last of the New Town Development Corporations and set about a demoralising sale of assets. By then, he wrote, he'd been 'wandering' the new towns for 40 years.

If on-the-spot observation, an urban anthropological approach, guided Colin, then everything he saw was informed by the prodigious reading of an auto-didact. *The Child in the City* is the fullest encapsulation of his thinking. As Shumi Bose notes, for him the city was a 'terrain of learning'. He introduces Kevin Lynch from the 'thriving academic industry' of behavioural psychology, weighing Lynch against Piaget, setting the options of the outside world against those of the space indoors. An admired philosopher, Gaston Bachelard, evoked a tissue of childhood impressions in *The Poetics of Space* ('the feel of the tiniest latch has remained in our hands'). Memories of 'experienced reality' were powerful beyond measure as Colin knew well.

As Colin wrote in *Influences*, though not trained as an architect, he had 'stayed on the drawing-board for 20 years'. He initially worked for an elderly architect, Sidney Caulfield, taking him at just one remove to the Gothic Revivalist John Loughborough Pearson but, more significantly, to W R Lethaby. His employer had been a student and colleague of Lethaby at the Central School of Arts and Crafts and became the Professor of Architecture at the school. It was in this and similar workplaces that Colin's fierce belief in the integrated place of environmental education within wider society had been honed.

There could have hardly been greater good fortune than to slip into architecture in a shrinking office doing no more than small repairs to bombed factory premises in east London. It left, I suspect, plenty of time for reading. Apart from essential technical volumes, Colin recalled, the office 'library' extended little further than Raymond Unwin's highly regarded book on town planning and three titles by Lethaby, including his examination of Philip Webb and a collection of essays. Colin Ward bracketed Lethaby with Walter Segal, at first glance 'worlds apart' but on further examination united by their formulation of an attitude 'to the art of building and life.' Both held a fierce commitment to the goal of social building and generous care for the right client. It was 'my friend' Gabriel Epstein (in whose office Shepheard Epstein he also worked for a period) who introduced him to the thinking of Martin Buber and the notion that the enduring tension between 'the social principle and the political principle' could only be resolved by 'autonomy' (his preferred term for 'anarchism').

At the end of his final chapter in *New Town, Home Town: The Lessons of Experience*, Colin surveyed the successes and failures of the programme from his vantage point in the early 1990s. He lingered, bitterly, on the 'saddest of all the shortcomings', when the 1940s Labour government chose not to honour the principle of the 'unearned increment' of site values as envisaged by Ebenezer Howard. By returning the revenue to the Treasury and centralised political control the compact was broken, and the autonomy that he and those he so admired and valued was shattered. That was compounded in the 1980s by the Conservative government's sale of social assets to private property speculators. The shocking absence of forward thinking, let alone vision, was, Colin wrote, the fault of successive political administrations rather than of the development corporations. These last paragraphs show a rare flash of anger as he muses on the 'lessons of experience' of the subtitle. And yet, even if living and working in a new town was no guarantee of happiness, he wrote, 'it has often eliminated some of the more avoidable kinds of misery'.

11. Colin Ward

A Quiet Voice of Dissent

Ruth Kinna

Like a lot of people, I suspect, I discovered Colin Ward when I picked up a copy of *Anarchy in Action* (1973). I was just starting postgraduate research on the concept of mutual aid. His modest claim that the book was an 'updating footnote' to Pyotr Kropotkin, the key figure in my planned dissertation, jumped off the page. But entangled by the multiple threads of Kropotkin's work, I struggled to make the connection between the update and the original. My second introduction was a short article written in the 60s about a ban that the BBC had slapped on a pop song. As I remember it, the song was apparently laden with risqué references to the rough handling of soft tomatoes. It had been deemed a little too rich in seaside humour for public consumption. Ward's wry commentary on the lofty virtue of the censors and their anxieties about the corruption of youth was funny. I copied out lengthy sections longhand, although the text was quite disconnected from the work I was doing. I still have my well-thumbed copy of *Anarchy in Action*, but the hand-written notes have disappeared and I can't remember either the publication details or the title of the song.

It took me a long time to work out that *Anarchy in Action* embraced the main lines of the theory I was attempting to investigate. Looking back, I can see why I was persuaded that the essays in the book were probably tangential to my historical study: the nod to *Mutual Aid*, the descriptions of everyday cooperation and resistance to bossy bureaucracy seemed to confirm Kropotkin's thesis without adding much to it. Although I filed the notes on the censorship essay, thinking that I might one day find an appropriate excuse to reference it, this reinforced my sense of a gap separating nineteenth century thinking from twentieth century politics.

I have since read a decent selection of Ward's work and have often turned to his succinct, careful writings on anarchism, utopia, violence, work and a score of other subjects to jumpstart my own thinking. Staring at a blank screen, it's reassuring to know that he's already been there and it's always instructive to cast an eye over the diverse literature he consulted when tackling a topic. But, as an admirer of his work, I also like to think that something Wardian has rubbed off on me. When I try to work out what this may be, I'm predictably led straight back to his work, notably his short book *Influences: Voices of Creative Dissent* (1991).

Influences describes anarchism by pairing appreciations of admired authors with a set of interrelated practical concerns: William Godwin and Mary Wollstonecraft for education, Alexander Herzen for politics, Kropotkin for economics, Martin Buber for society, William Lethaby and Walter Segal for architecture and Patrick Geddes and Paul Goodman for planning.

Describing each writer as an 'influence', Ward used the same word to refer to the external forces active on individuals as he did to describe the capacity of individuals to effect change. As an external force, 'influence' is a synonym for 'ideology' and 'socialisation'. On the one hand, it refers to the dissemination of pervasive, corrosive creeds and philosophies, for example nationalism and separatism. On the other, it suggests the complex and sometimes contrary norms and values that we all imbibe from friends, family and literature. As a capacity, influence is exerted by the publication of ideas or in actions. It is felt in the responses it provokes. In this sense, influence is about the things that people take from others. A leading contention of the book is that the expression of influence is integral to its exercise. Ideas can be expressed more or less angrily, encouragingly or abstractly and with more or less certainty or prescription. Observing that 'good people' have sometimes been inclined to sweet talk others into taking risky or impulsive actions, Ward especially commended writers who expressed themselves with gentleness. As he put it, he valued 'quiet voices of dissent and scepticism'.

It seems to me that *Influences* promotes a sort of jigsaw puzzle approach to anarchism. It invites multiple possible combinations of principles and authors as well as the modification of both. I like the book because it emphasises the mutability of principles, priorities and possibilities. Anarchism can be re-loaded to suit our preferences, contingencies; repeatedly disassembled and reconfigured in new arrangements of its discrete parts.

A similar flexibility informs Ward's view of utopia as a human space shaped by a 'million private dreams'. It is evident, too, in the pluralism he defended in *Anarchism: A Very Short Introduction* (2004), borrowing again from Martin Buber. This predisposition towards heterogeneity and multiplicity complicates the rubric 'No Gods! No Masters!'. In Ward's hands, it seems that anarchy may be compatible with multiple gods as well as the refusal of any unified system of belief. At the same time, it highlights the continuity of ideas and the existence of an intellectual tradition.

When I first read *Influences* I was especially comforted to learn that Ward 'endlessly quoted' other 'writers and propagandists' because he felt they were able to express his ideas and feelings more completely than he could himself. I don't think this meant that he considered himself a reporter rather than an interpreter, advocate or guide. But if he did, I think that description underplays his influence. To my mind, the significance of the comment lies in what it implies about the balance he struck between the hesitancy of quiet dissent and the assertiveness of political commentary.

When I first started reading his work, it did not occur to me that these spheres could be straddled or even merged. Re-reading *Anarchy in Action* through the lens of *Influences*, it seems a different book to the one I picked up in the early 1980s: not an 'updating footnote' to Kropotkin but an appeal, expressed in calm Kropotkinian terms, to reject and transform post-war liberal democracy. If Kropotkin had raised the alarm about the likely ramifications of state socialism and welfarism, Ward laid bare the Faustian pact at the heart of the 'warfare state'. *Anarchy in Action* matched Kropotkin's recommendations for learning and libertarian education by decrying the introduction of universal education as bureaucratic, regressive and elitist.

It took longer than it should have done for the penny to drop, but the influence I've taken from Ward's work is that anarchist histories are valuable for, and even vital to, the promotion of its practices, and that its practices are expressive of an incessantly changing history.

12. Arcadia Everywhere

David Knight

Colin Ward was the person who first explained the structure and character of the apparently banal and everyday places in which I and many others grew up. Through his extraordinary, multifaceted work, I was able to move from a childhood fascination with apparently unremarkable edgeland places – allotments, plotlands, suburbs, new towns – towards developing a form of practice that aims to be responsive to, and to have a positive impact upon, exactly these sorts of places.

I grew up on the suburban fringes of Shoreham-by-Sea in Sussex. The town was once a major shipbuilding town that dwarfed Brighton, its neighbour, but by the turn of the twentieth century it was a fairly sedate coastal town with a large shingle spit, known as the Beach, upon which a Napoleonic fort and some coastguard cottages had been built but very little else. By the 1920s, this shingle spit had transformed into an entirely new community of exiles from London and Brighton, living in informally built bungalows which were often made out of retired railway carriages from the nearby Lancing Carriage Works (where my grandfather worked), bought cheap and hauled across the river mouth by horses. The residents of Bungalow Town had a bohemian reputation – many of them were associated with a natural light film studio built on the beach in 1914, when feature films had to be made in greenhouses due to the light-processing capabilities of early film stock.

Over time, the architecture of Bungalow Town grew more ambitious, with many structures, such as a crenellated castle over five storeys, stretching the definition of 'bungalow', but at the same time the overall settlement grew increasingly 'normal', gaining telephone lines and made roads.

By the time Ward and Dennis Hardy visited Shoreham as part of their landmark study *Arcadia for All: The Legacy of a Makeshift Landscape* (1984), Shoreham Beach was unrecognisable as the eccentric settlement it had been up until World War Two. During wartime, 75 per cent of the beach had been cleared, ostensibly to create a more easily defensible coastline. Even before the outbreak of peace, the local council had become determined to prevent the old plotland structure from re-appearing and to create, in its place, a more respectable coastal suburb. It failed to do so several times, facing an increasingly militant local community across a Whitehall table, until the Town and Country Planning Act was passed in 1947. This new act, which created the national planning system as we now know it, effectively nationalised the right to build, on the assumption that most significant developments would be state-led. To enable this, it allowed local councils to compulsorily purchase any land needed to fulfil their local development plan.

Shoreham Beach was the first place in England and Wales to be compulsorily purchased using these new powers, and it was the first to receive a 'plan' for its state-led redevelopment, even though the plan wasn't even complete when the compulsory purchase was undertaken. Amid much argument and debate, this process initiated the version of Shoreham Beach we see today (and that I saw as a child) – a quiet and pleasant suburb, overwhelmingly residential, its many oddities mostly ironed out, barring one or two surviving railway carriages and a line of eclectic residential boats dotted along the river edge.

As a child I found this lost, bohemian civilisation fascinating. I began my researches into Bungalow Town at age 12 and have never really stopped, slowly evolving my interest to a more politicised and propositional one, framed by *Arcadia for All*'s exploration of what drove the local authority to stamp it out. The great tragedy of twentieth century planning in the UK is that the moment when it was most popular, most discussed on street corners and in the press, was the very moment when planning took a decisive shift away from the popular gaze and became something solely done for us by the state, an extreme position which is now being eroded not by popular activity but by the free market and by the ideology of austerity. In retrospect, these tensions, explored extensively through Ward's writing and thought, have fundamentally informed my work as an urban strategist, policy writer and planning theorist.

In Ward and Hardy's even-handed but penetrating analysis, the story of Bungalow Town is set out as a paradigmatic battle between a bureaucratic, centralising approach toward organisation and control and the popular, informal urge toward self-expression, emergence and mutual aid. We know what camp Ward is in, but works like *Arcadia for All* patiently and carefully take apart these structures and stories to give us powerful, politically useful narratives that define our apparently banal or overlooked environments. Beyond plotlands like Bungalow Town, Ward and David Crouch's (recently republished) work The *Allotment: Its Landscape and Culture* (1988, 2023) explores not just allotment gardening in its own terms but sets it as the fulcrum of far wider discourses and power struggles between the right to the city and the right to the countryside, between common access to growing land and enclosure. Through his work in education (notably *Streetwork: The Exploding School* (1973) and the *Bulletin of Environmental Education*, both with Anthony Fyson), as well as in his own studies of critically neglected landscapes and sites of resistance, Ward sets out a programme whereby our everyday environments are reframed as vital spaces of discovery and as the means by which a more just society, a more balanced environment, and a more enabled populace might yet be created.

13. Anarchism as Theory of Organisation

Martin Parker

Some radicals think they should be against 'organisation'. As if those who care about fundamental social change should be against formally specified relations, against the sort of ossification that is characteristic of corporations, political parties, states and business schools. This is related to the myth that anarchists are hopeless at organising themselves, and hypocrites if they even try. But what if Colin Ward was an organisation theorist, and anarchism was a theory of organising? In a 1966 essay which provides the title of this piece, Ward suggested that anarchist organisations should be voluntary, functional, temporary and small. We can learn a great deal from thinkers like him, particularly in times when we need new forms of organising to cope with the crises that face us.

Let's be clear: anarchists are not against organisation. Practical anarchists like Ward offer a sustained experiment in thinking about how a different life might be possible. It is easy to point to the problems of the present, and then to suggest (at the end of a series of complaints) that a new world is possible. What is much harder is to systematically imagine what those alternatives might look like, to turn opposition into proposals.

Anarchism is a rich stream of thought to stimulate such ideas because it is the first form of 'organisation theory' in which 'organisation' was assumed to be an open term. From classical anarchism onwards, the problem was precisely how we might live in the absence of the divine right of kings, the violence of the state, or the coercions of capital. Unlike theories of organisation which assume economic white man, managers, managed, the sale of labour, the superiority of markets and so on, anarchist organisation theory assumes very little. There might be a commitment to some version of individualism and/or community, but these generalities lead to actual descriptions of communes, federations, syndicalism, mutual aid, co-operatives or whatever.

Ward insists that all forms of organising are 'political', which is another way of saying that they are contested. They have upsides and downsides, and it simply isn't possible to say that there are some arrangements which are unambiguously good, and others that are unambiguously bad. Markets can be hugely helpful forms of reward and distribution in some circumstances, and communes can be oppressive and narrow places which crush individuality. Hierarchies of authority can be helpful too on occasion, particularly for making quick decisions, while democratic and popular education could easily reproduce sexist and racist ideas. There are always other ways of doing things.

It isn't always easy to decide what is 'alternative' because there are no forms of organisation which we can always and forever decide are good. There are plenty of accounts of institutions which start well but fall into bad habits, or become dominated by a cadre of leaders, or within which the excitement of the new becomes the atrophy of the old. Sometimes we could say that a noble goal has been displaced by a business logic: the logic of capitalism. This means that we always need to be wary about organising, even organising that appears 'alternative'.

Take, for example, education, which Ward wrote about often. Can we detach how something is being taught from why it is being taught? Many policy makers and students might argue that, for example, the university should be relevant to the economy and business, which typically seems to be a way of saying that it should fit students for jobs. In that case, the university is merely a means to get a degree certificate. But it is very difficult to argue that the end of certifying potential employees is the *only* purpose of the university, simply because the means are crucial to achieve the end. The process of learning is what we learn, and the certificate you get when you leave states that you have undergone that process, not simply that you have learned certain facts and can repeat them. The educational means are the end, unless we argue that a university is only there to award degree certificates in return for money.

Or, consider decision-making. Within conventional organisations, decisions are made by those with power and status. We could say that a decision is a means to an end and having 'managers' make those decisions is a means that ensures that getting to the end is speedier and more efficient. Perhaps, but as many anarchists have argued, we could treat collective decision-making as an end in itself. If the intention of the organisation's members is to take decisions slowly and democratically, then the very process of organising in a particular way becomes its own end, as well as a means by which other goals might be achieved. Such organising is prefigurative in the sense that it attempts to bring new forms of social relationships into being. A distinction between means and end, cause and effect, which seems quite secure in common sense, begins to look rather suspicious, and politically loaded, within a form of organising which attempts to build a new world in the shell of the old.

We should always be suspicious if someone tells us that there is no alternative, no choice, and that we should be 'realistic'. The end point of many arguments against change is that things have to be like this because of 'the market', or 'the bottom line', or 'human nature' which are usually assertions that suit those who wish to defend the present state of affairs. Ward and other anarchists think that no particular forms of human organising are inevitable, and that there are always choices about means, ends and the relations between them. For example, if we imagine the university as a mechanism for producing the future, then perhaps it can produce different futures and different sorts of people to inhabit them.

Opening up the politics and possibilities of organising like this doesn't solve our problems. It makes things more difficult because we can no longer admit arguments about inevitability and instead we have to justify our choices. These will have to be reasons which encompass both means and ends, processes and purposes, and rest upon some sort of idea about the kinds of society and people we wish to encourage. Visions of a different form of social order are central to the judgements we might make concerning what is alternative and what is mainstream, about community and coercion, fair exchange and appropriation.

In the closing paragraph of his 1907 essay 'Anarchism, Individualism and Organization', Errico Maletesta said that 'everyone organises themselves – organisers and anti-organisers. Only those who do little or nothing can live in isolation, contemplating. This is the truth; why not recognise it.' He is suggesting that we should think of organising as a kind of politics made durable. Our current versions of management, leaders, employees and so on constitute a set of assumptions which are solidified in organisational configurations. These aren't necessary and inevitable arrangements, dictated by the structure of our genes or the invisible hand of the market. Rather than seeing organising as a technical matter, something to be left to experts with MBAs, we can understand it as a way of working through the complex issues of being human with other humans and hence a responsibility and possibility for all of us. Politics has much to learn from anarchism because it makes organisation radically contingent.

For example, if we claim that democracy – the rule of the people – is a value that we care about then we might reasonably ask why so many decisions in workplaces are taken autocratically, by a small minority? Arguments from expertise or efficiency might work in particular cases – such as when a doctor uses their expertise to diagnose a medical problem – but this is not the case in most situations. Why assume that all forms of organisation need a class of people called 'managers', and that these people should be paid so much more than the workers? Why are these managers appointed and not elected? Why assume that the people who work for a company will be different from the people who own it? Why not have workers or trade union representatives sitting on boards of directors? Why do shareholders have votes but not employees, members of local communities or customers?

Once these sorts of questions and many others are opened up, it is difficult to get them back in the box. This moves us away from thinking that organising is what happens *after* decisions have been taken, and that it can be left to other people. In societies with a complex division of labour, professional politicians and policy makers, global supply chains and gigantic corporations, it is not surprising we should believe this. Most often, the responsibility does not seem to be ours when we swipe a credit card, buy some shoes, or tick a box on a ballot paper. We make a choice and someone else organises things for us.

In response to this, Ward encourages us to think locally, to think small because any meaningful use of words like 'community', 'sustainability' and so on must refer to a particular group of people with names and faces. Otherwise the words are merely hopeful labels with no reference to the times and places where we live our lives. One of the features of the 'there is no alternative' argument is to point to forces outside the local which constrain decision-making. 'If it was up to me…'; 'in an ideal world…'; 'if we don't do this…' are all phrases which deny local agency and point to a framework which means that things just have to be like they are. Other people and things – 'head office', 'the market', 'the customer' – can be given the responsibility. But this buck passing has a cost in terms of the way it prevents us from seeing that these responsibilities are ours, too, and that we could do things in different ways. That is why many radical alternatives confront us with the local, with what is in front of our noses, because it is there that we spend most of our lives.

Not that any of this is easy, because simply imagining that the world could be different merely builds castles in the air. Ward and other anarchists provide us with a cookery book in which the arguments provide some ideas and inspiration. Browsing through the recipes, you are not being told what to make, when to make it and how to eat it, but are being encouraged to experiment with autonomy, solidarity and possibility.

14. Resonating with Colin Ward

Sol Pérez-Martínez

As a Chilean architect, it still surprises me – as well as others – that I dedicated five years of my life to research the writings, projects and people surrounding Colin Ward, a British anarchist writer who only has one book available in Spanish. Encountering Ward's work in 2015 not only changed the way I research and write, but also my approach to everyday tasks, from planting herbs on the balcony to choosing the place I live. Researching Ward introduced me to a network of inspiring 'Wardian' friends – starting with his wife: the educator and writer Harriet Ward – who have expanded my thinking and enriched my understanding of Britain. Ward has become a central reference in my work, helping me feel more comfortable with my approach to action-based lower-case politics; his ideas operating as an ethical compass to navigate a world in need of reparation.

As an avid reader, it is not often that I remember the location of the first time I encountered a book, but with Ward's *The Child in the City* (1978) I have a clear mental image. It was the first year of my PhD at University College London and I was sitting in the second floor of the library of the Institute of Education (IoE), a brutalist building in clear need of repair, with brown carpets, frosty windows overlooking a quiet inner garden, the chairs upholstered in a bright blue fabric from the 1980s. Always busy, filled with educators, teachers-to-be and their primary-coloured materials, the IoE was a foreign environment where I felt at odds after spending most of my life at architecture schools. I had a pile of books on my desk and held my head in my hand while endlessly sifting through the pages, looking for references that combined architecture and education. *The Child in the City* stood out from the others. Its large format cover with a black and white photograph of a child playing, and its bright yellow font, worked as a visually attractive pamphlet. Inside it, Ann Golzen's striking photographs portrayed a type of childhood long gone, where children were free to roam and explore. But it was reading Ward which finally made me sit up straight. I felt that for the first time, after a year of research, someone understood what I was looking for: a way of helping others become involved and take ownership of the environment around them. Ward's ideas struck a chord.

Before arriving in the UK, I lived in Santiago de Chile, running an architectural practice with two firm partners while teaching architectural history. As a young firm, we were keen to move from private to public projects to help Chile recover from the 2010 earthquake that destroyed part of the country's public infrastructure. In 2011, we won our first public competition to build Malleco's town hall. Soon after this, we won a second public competition to build a high school in the town of Contulmo. I trace the origins of this research back to the first consultation meeting of the public school, held between the government representatives, the community and the architecture firms involved. As the project leader, I found the experience of the participation processes coordinated by the Ministry of Public Works tokenistic and problematic due to the school community's lack of involvement. I was surprised by how communities, when given the opportunity, struggled to express their design preferences and preferred to follow the opinion of 'experts' and authorities. This experience led me to question existing procedures and to search for practices to increase the involvement of citizens.

Stepping away from practice into academia after developing these two public projects offered me a period to reflect on my six years of experience in our architecture firm. I questioned our agency as architects during the projects' development, our relationship with the communities we had served, and how people related to the built environment throughout the design process. I started my doctoral project with the intuition that it was the educational system and its infrastructure that alienated children and adults from becoming involved in local architecture and planning. To help solve this, I wanted to find examples of educational projects that could help increase citizen involvement in the built environment.

When I started my research, there were no built environment education projects in Chile. Research confirms that the cultural blackout created by 17 years of Augusto Pinochet's dictatorship weakened civic engagement in Chile. How, then, to help people become involved in and take ownership of their local surroundings? I decided to look to international examples, to find initiatives that combined education and architecture. Although there were interesting initiatives in Finland, Spain and the USA, I decided to concentrate on the UK as an epicentre of architectural design and leading architecture schools. Many British contemporary educational projects claimed to encourage civic engagement but concentrated in creativity, which, though important, is not the same as political participation or involvement. Ward's work was the first example of an educational project that had politics at its core.

Ward dedicated his life to investigating the relation between people and their environment. Physical space for Ward was important because it crystallised social and political ideas that at times are hard to grasp, like inequality or power. According to Ward, an education grounded in the physical world allows us to relate to the local, connecting to meaningful experiences in a shared reality. This is not to define a parochial view of reality or to incentivise nationalist sentiments; Ward proposed a local view with a global awareness, following Patrick Geddes' maxim of 'think global, act local'. Ward's writings in his journal, the *Bulletin of Environmental Education*, the *Town and Country Planning Journal* and his many books encouraged architects, planners, teachers, geographers and artists, among others, to collaborate and deliver built environment education projects. One of these projects was the Urban Studies Centres Movement, with almost 40 centres for built environment education across the UK.

There were two things that surprised me during the research process. The first was how a social movement that spanned more than 20 years, creating almost 50 organisations, with multiple physical centres and publishing extensively, could be overlooked by recent history, even in one of the wealthiest nations of the world. Finding the term 'Urban Studies Centre' in Ward's The *Child in the*

City and researching its origins revealed a wealth of stories of dozens of people who promoted more equitable built environments in Britain. How many other stories of voluntary and civil organisations working with architecture and the built environment are not recorded? How many practitioners are starting from scratch when there are experiences that could inform their projects?

The second surprise was what I described in my notes intuitively as resonance, the feeling of vibrating at the same frequency with others despite different cultures, ages, languages or locations, amplifying a common aim, either face to face or through writing. The metaphor of resonance is often used in social movement studies and sociology to describe how, as Terence McDonnell, Christopher Bail and Iddo Tavory write in 'A Theory of Resonance' (*Sociological Theory*, 2017) 'certain discourses, messages or other cultural objects have an advantage over others because they fit – or resonate with – prevailing cultural worldviews of the audiences who receive them'. For sociologist Hartmut Rosa, resonance is a relational, emergent, situated phenomenon, when something affects us and produces an emotional response or action. In *Resonance. A Sociology of Our Relationship to the World* (2016) Rosa describes resonance as 'a form of world-relation, in which subject and world meet and transform each other'. Therefore, resonance needs difference and interaction, not harmony, to effect a 'transformative appropriation of difference' (see her 'The Idea of Resonance as a Sociological Concept' in *Global Dialogue*, 2018).

I confess that the first time I read Ward's criticism of architects and planners, it made me feel uncomfortable because it challenged my training, but at the same time I felt his ideas offered a response to civic engagement in architecture that was outside the comfort zone of my discipline. Ward's writing style aimed to resonate and effect change. Resonance is important for advocacy because, as Vincent Miller says in 'Resonance as a Social Phenomenon (*Sociological Research Online*, 2015) it 'allows activist reporting and storytelling to strike a chord with readers, thereby encouraging certain kinds of (moral) evaluations in audiences'. Resonance, say McDonnell, Bail and Tavory, offers a 'creative moment wherein actors find novel solutions to their problems or extend familiar solutions to unfamiliar problems'. Though anarchism was unfamiliar to me, Ward's ideas seemed a novel solution to the recurring problem of disengagement from the built environment. Drawing on Ward's work and his network of collaborators, I learned that civic engagement in architecture and urban change is not a one-way process where architects or planners teach citizens to engage, but a two-way process where citizens, educators and architects learn from each other.

I started researching Ward's work with the aim of finding practices to educate young people to care and get involved in taking ownership of their environment, but as a result this research has educated me to de-centre my position as an architect, to navigate the friction and conflict of collaboration, to find a common ground and to learn where I stand socially and politically. As an architect, Ward has taught me that the key for civic engagement in architecture and the built environment is to learn in collaboration with others. My research into Ward's work and his network offers stories of how this collaboration happened in the past and the practices that can allow this collaboration to happen again.

15. Play, Education, Creativity and Activism

The Legacies of Colin Ward

Martin Stott

I first came across Colin Ward, as so many people did, through his writings, as a teenage school student. I was 16 when his Penguin Education topic book *Violence* was published in 1970. In the context of everything from the Vietnam War to violence on football terraces, the connections made were both inspiring and terrifying. *Work*, which came out a couple of years later in 1972, had even more of an impact, introducing me to William Morris ('A factory as it might be') in an accessible, informal and thought-provoking way. So in 1978, when I started working at the Town and Country Planning Association (TCPA) after graduating in geography and training in town planning, I could hardly believe my luck to be pitched into an organisation where geography, planning, the built environment and a certain kind of anarchic informality infused the organisation. I was knocking around the left libertarian circles of South London at the time, setting up and co-editing the magazine *South Circular*, a thorn in the side of the local Labour Party establishment, and sharing with TCPA colleague Rob Cowan a 'hard to let' flat on the 15th floor of a tower block on the Brandon Estate in Walworth, which ended up being the set for anti-hero Ray's flat in the cult punk rock movie about The Clash, *Rude Boy* (1980). At the time, I was learning to navigate both London and independent living, and the diary I started the previous year was a useful way of processing the experiences and practising my writing.

Not surprisingly, I was drawn to Colin, then well into his stride at the TCPA's Education Unit. Between the excitement of watching editions of the *Bulletin of Environmental Education* (*BEE*) being put together, and undertaking various dogsbody roles for the Association, such as helping organise conferences and launch events (including for Colin's *The Child in the City* (1978)) I was roped into writing occasional short book reviews and similar for *BEE*. I was, at 23, a representative of 'youth'. Long lunch hours, smoking breaks and good conversation were very much *du jour*. So Colin took me under his wing and plied me with back copies of *Anarchy*: my diary on 8 April 1978 records him giving me 'about a dozen copies' over lunch, he being 'quietly reflective on life', in the Institute for Contemporary Arts (ICA) café, conveniently located just underneath the TCPA. Over the next 18 months or so, Colin gifted me copies of books he thought were important for me to read, including his own *Anarchy in Action* (1973) and *Housing: An Anarchist Approach* (1976). I was in a position to report to him from the front line of the burgeoning anti-nuclear, anti-racist, green and peace movements including the Anti-Nazi League march to Victoria Park in 1978, skirmishes with the National Front in Walworth, and the occupation of the Torness nuclear power station site in Scotland in 1979, with its various 'affinity groups' and non-violent direct action training sessions. My book *The Nuclear Controversy* was published by the TCPA in 1980.

Colin and his Education Unit teammates Eileen Adams and Anthony Fyson inhabited a strange (for a conventional office – but then this was no conventional office) mezzanine area in the rather grand surroundings of Carlton House Terrace, and what I recorded as 'superb banter' could be 'carried on over the balcony' (1 November 1978). On the death of TCPA guiding spirit Sir Fredrick Osborn (FJO), there was 'some ribaldry' as attempts were made to find out how to organise a memorial meeting for an atheist, with 'Colin producing gems on FJO and his life, and also on previous memorial meetings he had been to' (2 November 1978).

The ICA was a source of cultural enrichment that complemented the TCPA, the two in those days being joined by a narrow stairway not open to the public but offering free access, presumably a fire escape. So a lunchtime talk by Raymond Williams was followed by a trip to the cinema in Wardour Street that evening with Colin to see Mike Dibb's newly released film version of *The Country and the City* (15 February 1979). That spring and summer, as Colin's involvement with the TCPA wound down before retirement from the Education Unit, our many conversations revolved around the wider anarchist movement, the emerging Green Movement and planning and the built environment. A steady flow of books from his library were pressed upon me, including Murray Bookchin's *Post-Scarcity Anarchism* (1971), Paul Goodman's *Communitas* (1947) and *Growing Up Absurd* (1960) and Martin Buber's *Paths in Utopia*

(1949) to supplement the points discussed. William Morris made an appearance, too, and it was fitting that a major exhibition at the ICA in 1984, *William Morris Today*, included in its accompanying publication an essay by Colin entitled 'Morris as Anarchist Educator'. One day in mid-1978, Colin came into the office and called to me in some excitement, clutching an Italian anarchist-inspired rural development magazine, and pointed to an article of mine about agriculture in China. Much amusement followed when we realised that it was an article lifted – without permission of course – from the TCPA's own Journal that I had written the previous year.

While writing my book for the TCPA, I was also trying my hand at shorter pieces for the TCPA journal and *BEE* and, as I gradually grew in confidence both as a writer and in the clarity of my opinions, for other green and radical publications including *Vole, Peace News, Undercurrents, The Leveller, Co-op News, Marxism Today, Built Environment* and, of course, *South Circular*, where I reviewed *The Child in the City* (1978). Colin's guidance on tone, length and style were invaluable. One watch word of his about book reviewing has stayed with me: 'If you can't find anything positive to say about a book, Martin, don't say anything at all. Return it and get the editor to ask someone else to review it. Put yourself in the author's shoes.'

Around the same time as Colin left London for Suffolk, I moved to Oxford to work for the Political Ecology Research Group. As a worker co-op it was also pretty free-wheeling and allowed me the space both to continue writing and to explore some of the 'life themes' I had absorbed from my time at the

TCPA with Colin. Looking back, two stand out and overlap: exploring 'makeshift landscapes', or 'edgelands' as they later became known, and children's self-expression and play. My much-thumbed copy of *The Child in the City* was an essential guide and inspiration – not least for its photographs. It wasn't long before I had established a thriving set of Woodcraft Folk groups with fellow co-op and peace activists. They allowed opportunities for adults and children to explore the local townscape and landscape: spotting gargoyles town trail-style on the university's colleges, political education at the annual 'Levellers Day' festival in Burford, day-long hikes and wild camping in the Cotswolds at a time when 'right to roam' was a salient issue, and discovering the joys of growing and nature on local allotments. As well as cultivating an allotment, I took to photographing them, and material from my 1991 exhibition, *Earthly Paradise: People and Landscapes on Allotments*, was used by Roger Deakin in his TV programme *The Ballad of the Ten Rod Plot* (1992). For me, play, education, creativity and activism merged as my daughters grew; freedom as a social activity in practice. I was fortunate.

Distance and parental responsibilities, not to mention a new job in the emerging environmental field in local government, led to a rich correspondence on these subjects over the next couple of decades. These were supplemented by occasional visits to Oxford by Colin, usually to lecture to his friend Nabeel Hamdi's classes on informal settlements and the like at Oxford Polytechnic, or visits by me to Suffolk, or more often get-togethers in London on the fringes of TCPA events. Writing remained an important element of my life nurtured by Colin, including a column in the TCPA journal, still going after 37 years, and an edited book with David Crouch, *City Fields, Country Gardens: Allotment Essays* (1998), which I somehow managed to eke out between other commitments, and which Colin joyfully reviewed in *Freedom*.

Looking back to those days at the TCPA and in South London in the late 1970s, I had no idea just how significant and formative they would be. Many people and events have influenced me, but Colin Ward was the person who gave them a focus and coherence that has lasted the whole of my adult life.

16. Colin Ward and the Sound of Anarchy

Stuart White

One day in 1980, aged 14 years old, a school friend lent me his copy of a record that had just come out. It was a split single by the punk bands Poison Girls and Crass.

Crass' 'Bloody Revolutions', one side of the record, is an anarchist and pacifist critique of the Marxist theory of revolution. Crass weren't against revolution – but they wanted a revolution of 'anarchy and peace'.

The Poison Girls' track 'Persons Unknown' added to my curiosity.

In the main part of the track, singer Vi Subversa pictures a state that oversees its many diverse subjects, seeking out the 'persons unknown' who constitute a threat. The guitars swing and spiral with growing tension as Subversa lists the many faces of this threatening public before reaching the final lines: 'Flesh and blood are who we are/Flesh and blood are what we are/Flesh and blood are who we are/Our cover is blown…' Beyond the labels we use to distinguish and separate ourselves there is a shared humanity and vulnerability – a basis for solidarity.

At this point, the song fades out…Then, unexpectedly, the music starts again, purely instrumental now, gradually shifting into a purposive pulse overlaid with crisp but dreamy synths.

The tension of the preceding part of the song has been resolved. I decided that this last minute or so of the track must be the sound of the world 'after the revolution' – the sound of 'anarchy and peace'. It sounded great. I wanted to live there. And I still do.

Yet, if this was the sound of anarchy, it was hard to imagine what 'anarchy' looks like. How does it work? The Sex Pistols' 'Anarchy in the UK' (1976) called for us to 'Get pissed! Destroy!' But it was hard to see how that really amounted to an alternative vision of how society might work.

Over the next few years, mass unemployment, riots in English cities, IRA bombing campaigns, cruise missiles and Falklands war jingoism gave teenagers in my generation a lot to think about. Fascinated both by anarchism and by the Marxism that Crass were criticising, the local public library, a ten-minute walk away, provided books on Marxism and anarchism. I helped to found my local branch of the Campaign for Nuclear Disarmament (CND). In Coventry city centre, I chatted with the scary, very sure-of-themselves newspaper sellers of the Revolutionary Communist Tendency – soon to be Revolutionary Communist Party. It must have been in The Wedge bookshop in Coventry that I found *Freedom* newspaper and Colin Ward's book *Anarchy in Action* (1973).

Ward's book puzzled me. If we assume that 'anarchy' is the focus of a revolution which will totally remake the social world, then we need to know how a whole society can work as an 'anarchy'. But *Anarchy in Action* doesn't try to explain this. It has discussions of things like self-help groups, housing and adventure playgrounds. But this seemed fragmentary and to miss or evade the challenge of explaining 'anarchy'. Finding no answer to my questions in Ward's book, or in other anarchist thinkers, it was easy to give up on anarchism as unrealistic.

Studying philosophy, politics and economics at Oxford University, and then doing graduate work in political theory, my thinking became framed by Marxism and liberalism, trying to work out their mutual strengths and weaknesses and the possibilities of creative combination. Privileged to become an academic, working in political theory, this became my research agenda. As a citizen, it defined my politics.

However, that final, uplifting minute in the Poison Girls' track remained evocative. Over the years, in the UK and USA, I collected more of Ward's books, especially his writings on housing. It seemed necessary to go back to his work. There was something important in it.

Gradually, I realised that I was looking in his work for an answer to a question that Ward thinks is precisely the wrong question to ask.

If we ask, 'How will a whole society work on anarchist lines?', we will inevitably end up with no satisfactory answer. Ward's point is that anarchism should not be understood as a social philosophy that is practically totalising in this sense. Indeed, in Ward's view, no social or political philosophy can plausibly claim to offer a total practical answer to social organisation. All societies use multiple organisational methods. To paraphrase Ward, the planned society of mid-twentieth century Communism and the free market society of the early twenty-first century tech-bro 'libertarian' are both utopia-dystopias, inevitably forced in practice to draw on methods that are contrary to what they proclaim. They would collapse if they didn't.

By the same token, look around and you will find that some problems are being solved, right now, by use of anarchist techniques of mutual aid and collective self-help. Anarchy is already 'in action' – in the squatters' group or the 12-step group or the consumer or workers' co-operative. Indeed, anarchy was there in the organisation of Crass Records and in the way the proceeds of the 'Bloody Revolutions'/'Persons Unknown' single were used to set up the (alas, short-lived) Wapping Autonomy Centre.

Now this point might seem too deflationary; to rescue the relevance or respectability of 'anarchy' at the price of making it a rather limited sphere of social life. Ward's argument, though, is that the anarchy already in action is a bridgehead from which we should try to build further anarchic spaces. Our society currently solves certain problems using anarchist techniques. What other problems can it solve using these techniques, cutting down its use of state-bureaucratic or market-based methods? How can we apply anarchic organisational principles, say, to food production? To the design and delivery of healthcare? To neighbourhood democracy? To the management of firms?

The idea of a completely anarchic society remains, for Ward, a standard against which to evaluate our society – a society is more or less good based on how close it is to this standard. But at the same time, Ward suggests that we don't need to worry about whether anarchy can work as a complete model of social organisation. Just focus on how we can use anarchist methods to expand the sphere of anarchy here and now. In this way, we can make our society more free and more equal – and, perhaps, more joyful.

While Ward's approach is incremental, this does not mean that it lacks revolutionary edge. Expanding anarchy pragmatically may well require that we act in revolutionary ways in some situations, confronted by specific legal and political obstacles which make this necessary.

Thanks in large part to Ward, my research agenda as an academic is now to integrate insights from Marxism, liberalism *and* anarchism. How can this perspective contribute to meeting our contemporary challenges?

One of Ward's contributions was to identify ways in which anarchism can strike creative partnerships with social democratic initiatives such as the post-war new towns. This is relevant today as we think about the urgent challenges of climate justice and the imperative of a global Green New Deal. A Green New Deal implies a strong role for the state in mobilising investment towards renewables and energy efficiency. But it also needs multiple anarchic ventures, such as community gardens, neighbourhood recycling hubs and energy co-operatives, all part of the 'commons'.

The picture of society this suggests is not simply 'anarchy'. But Ward's work can help us appreciate the constructive, convivial potential of anarchy in this situation. For me, Ward's work helps to bridge fear and anger at climate change, and the global injustices it is causing, to the exciting sense of possibility and renewal suggested by that Poison Girls track in 1980.

17. 'A marginal person like me'?

Patrick Wright

Garden cities, housing co-operatives, popular planning initiatives, squats (both short-life and long)… I can still hear Colin Ward pulling examples out of an apparently infinite store of remembered initiatives and projects, as he explained the long and varied history of mutual aid from across a table in the YMCA canteen in Great Russell Street, Bloomsbury. In those days, his white hair was still fronted by the yellowed quiff of a freelancer who had spent decades smoking at a clattering typewriter. His curiosity and enthusiasm were impressive, as was the grittiness with which he – certainly no bomb-thrower – pushed back against his too kind, even dreamy, reputation as 'the gentle anarchist'.

Our first meeting took place in 1985. I was working at the National Council for Voluntary Organisations, which then still aligned itself with Lord Beveridge's *Voluntary Action*, published in 1948 as a partly corrective sequel to the more famous Beveridge Report of 1942. With the new Social Service State attending to matters of bread and health, the Liberal peer had now declared it time to recover the ways of the great nineteenth century reformers who were driven less by the business motive than by a spirit of freedom, brotherhood and common purpose. These pioneers had shown the voluntary way of putting unhappiness out of the world and creating a future in which human society could at last become 'a friendly society – an Affiliated Order of branches…'.

By the mid-eighties, Margaret Thatcher and her government were engaged in a much blunter rolling back of the Welfare State, seen less as a virtuous instrument of relief than as a disabling Soviet-like encroachment on national life. In one field after another, voluntary sector organisations were being invited to step into the gap as government-funded service providers.

I was part of a small unit formed to help such agencies deal with the organisational challenges of this new version of welfare pluralism. We didn't have to look far to see that the very idea of a single voluntary sector was itself a state-born abstraction. Some occupants of this category were indeed consolidated agencies, already running various services. Others could hardly have been more different. Instead of a unified sector there was actually an extraordinary mixture of associations operating at different scales, across many different fields of interest, and presenting diverse types or degrees of organisation too. There were indeed service-providing charities, but also cooperatives and campaigns, the latter often gathered around a single cause and led by a founding figure whose charisma could be a strength one minute and a curse the next. There were mutual aid initiatives, created by a membership with a common concern and often more like localised communities, informal improvisations, or temporary projects than hierarchically structured organisations. While all sought to be effective in their chosen ways, a good number were justifiably suspicious of the idea of importing managerial techniques with the help of business consultants who struggled to recognise that there could ever be such a thing as an effective not-for-profit organisation.

Colin Ward was among those we contacted as we looked around for people who might help us reach a more adequate understanding of the organisational challenges faced by these less formally structured organisations in the new funding climate. There seemed to be nowhere in time or space that Ward hadn't been in his search for examples of mutual aid in action.

He had taken on the Beveridge Report of 1942 during his time as the editor of *Freedom*, insisting that the esteemed Liberal peer had overlooked the older mutual aid traditions that had long played a vital role in British health care and should, he believed, be maintained within the NHS. He had also commended 'anarchy in action' as he had found it in various domains of present social administration. He had seen some nice outbreaks in housing. Having championed squatting and the tenants' movement over previous decades, he would soon be commending the success of the Weller Streets housing co-op in Liverpool, recognised as the first housing co-op to be designed, built and owned by its residents (who worked in consultation with the architect Bill Halsall).

In many of his articles and books, Ward was concerned with recovering the memory of overtaken achievements before they were completely lost to the past. He had insisted on the original ambitions of the village colleges founded from the 1930s onwards by the Chief Education Officer of Cambridgeshire, Henry Morris, and also of the post-war new towns (he would be damning about the locking and privatisation of the once communal shopping building in Milton Keynes). Colin also told me about *Street Work:*

the Exploding School (1973). Writing with Anthony Fyson under the aegis of his then employer, the Town and Country Planning Association, he had suggested that urban schools should come up with their own version of the field trip. Instead of occasionally taking inner city children into the countryside to gawp at stately homes, he wanted teachers, architects and others to help students learn from their own environments.

Ward maintained this enquiry through the 1980s, producing a trio of books that are unique among the probings of British experience carried out in the Thatcher period. While others concentrated on economic and political questions as they were fought out at Westminster, Ward was roaming the country, tracing the popular mutual aid and self-help initiatives that had marked altogether more marginal places. The first and perhaps most influential and effective of these three books, is surely *Arcadia for All* (1984). Written together with Dennis Hardy, the planner and historian of English utopias who would go on to become Vice Chancellor of the University of Seychelles, this celebration of the makeshift plotland landscapes of derided places such as Canvey, Jaywick and Sheppey was a challenge to readers reluctant to think twice about their hostility to the despoliation of the British countryside.

Two years later, Ward and Hardy applied a similar attention to the British holiday camp, recovering the popular origins of places that may since have been taken over, fenced in and commercialised by big operators such as Butlin's or Warner's. He then teamed up with David Crouch to produce a book about allotments, reconnecting them to a long history of popular land use. In the 1920s, so readers would learn, German Marxists had condemned anarchist allotment holders for their 'flight from the class struggle'. For Ward and his colleague, however, allotments were places where the 'gift relationship' extended to acts of cross-cultural collaboration such as occurred when Asian allotment-holders in the Midlands introduced other initially suspicious holders to methods of irrigation that would keep their crops alive despite hosepipe bans.

People have wondered how Ward managed to hold on to his sense of optimism. If he managed to do that, it was surely because he did not conceive of the anarchist impulse as a unified political programme or a utopian blueprint for some more benign future. He came to see it instead as 'a mode of human organisation' rooted in the requirements and social aspirations of everyday life. As such, it was continually re-emerging alongside and in critical tension with 'the dominant authoritarian trends'.

So what did I and my then colleagues learn about organisation from these fascinating conversations? If I remember correctly, Colin nodded in recognition when I mentioned how vicious politically virtuous and, allegedly, caring organisations could be in their internal disputes. The more informal the organisation, the more brutal things could get, as we had already learned from the American feminist Jo Freeman's well-known article on 'The Tyranny of Structurelessness'. Understanding that, as he surely did from his own years in the service of anarchist projects, did not mean that Colin would ever countenance the thought that management of the conventional kind that then seemed increasingly to rule the world, might provide any part of the answer. Writing in the early seventies, Ward had quoted from the economist Robert Oakeshott, who had announced that one of the 'preconditions of success' necessary for a thriving co-operative venture, was the adoption of 'a management team… not inferior to that a conventional enterprise would enjoy'. Such terms, he had added, were not 'particularly acceptable to anarchists'. I don't think he ever changed his mind about that.

He was, after all, the very opposite of a management thinker of the type then beginning to offer voluntary organisations remedial tips about team-work or target-setting. On other matters, however, he was always generous with suggestions. I must have mentioned a hostile review of my first book (*On Living in an Old Country*) published earlier that year since I remember him advising me to take the approach recommended by Paul Goodman, the New York author of *Growing Up Absurd* and other anarchist works: 'Don't count the shit, count the [column] inches'. He offered more personally expressed advice when I suggested I might soon join him in the freelance life: 'Don't give up the day job!' he warned, with a look of some urgency in his eye. As for the prevailing theme of that now overtaken age, I can only remember one occasion when Colin told me anything connected to money. He was, if I remember rightly, talking about his Anglo-Italian anarchist friend Vernon Richards, a former editor of *Freedom* magazine who had spent his later years living as an organic small-holder in Suffolk. Colin had one day asked him about the unexpected smile on his face. Richards explained that he had reached the age when the state pension started paying out and had never known such riches in his life.

18. Schools
Without Walls
Ken Worpole

I first met Colin Ward in the spring of 1973 when, as a teacher at Hackney Downs School, I attended an in-service training course at the Inner London Education Authority (ILEA) Urban Studies Centre in Islington. Colin had been invited to speak about his current interests, having with Anthony Fyson just finished *Streetwork: The Exploding School* (1973), shortly to be published, and now working on the book which would become his landmark study, *The Child in the City* (1978). Claiming to have been bored at school himself, Colin recalled that once outdoors in the street he became curious about everything, which had led to him becoming a keen advocate of the idea of 'schools without walls', in which students found out how everyday life worked by direct study: trips to the local fire station, sewage farm, rubbish tip, railway station and signal box, farm and factory. Already at this time, Ivan Illich, an Austrian priest and a major critic of state education, had published *De-Schooling Society* in 1971. This proved to be a rallying cry to educationists across the world to reinvent mass public education as a community-based network of learning hubs for all ages and all abilities, with extended links into local everyday life and community – a little of what the Cambridge 'village college' initiative under Henry Morris had anticipated in the 1930s.

Following that first meeting, Colin and I began to correspond, and since both of us wrote for *New Society* – though he was a regular columnist with his own byline and I an occasional contributor – we began to meet from time to time. Eventually my wife Larraine and I got to know Colin and Harriet Ward as friends. There were other shared interests, notably in Colin's enthusiasm for 'junk playgrounds', or adventure playgrounds as they were more sedately called, where the principles of self-build and free play meshed seamlessly. Both Larraine and I had been involved in setting up an adventure playground on the Moulsecoomb Estate in Brighton in 1966, and were still involved in several play projects in Hackney where we now lived.

Colin's enthusiasm for the life of the street not only informed his pedagogy (though I doubt if he would have used that word), it also formed the very core of his anarchism. As Sophie Scott-Brown noted in her biography, *Colin Ward and the Art of Everyday Anarchy* (2022): 'For Colin Ward, anarchy was ordinary, everywhere, and always in action. It happened on city streets, allotments and around kitchen tables, in village halls, town squares and pub snugs. It went about its business quietly, beneath and beyond official notice.'

Such ideas were becoming part of the post-war social policy zeitgeist, particularly across war-torn Europe, though it was to prove a sadly short-lived but hopeful era of child-centred urban design. This was evident in the city-wide street playground designs of Aldo van Eyck in Amsterdam, and the 'junk playground' innovations of C T Sørenson in Denmark, both initiatives of the 1940s. Such experiments were supported culturally by a new wave of street photography which emphasised the street as the locus of social life, particularly for children. Photographers Helen Levitt in New York and Roger Mayne in London both produced highly influential books portraying children at play in the streets of overcrowded neighbourhoods – where they had become the temporary lords of misrule – but there was a similar enthusiasm for photographing children at play across the world, helping reinforce a mood of post-war political optimism.

To my mind it was Colin's greatest achievement – to put the unique lifeworld of the child at the centre of anarchist philosophy, thereby creating a major break with traditional left-wing ideology (proletkult culture) that located the male industrial worker as the sole agent and subject of revolutionary social change. Whether he had read Sartre or not I don't know, but many years ago I remember reading that the French existentialist philosopher once angrily retorted to a doctrinaire comrade that people are born not as workers but as children: if there was such a thing as an essentialist identity, then that most likely belonged to that formed in childhood, shaping the rest of their lives.

Such counter-intuitive understandings of the street as a public space, in an age when the car was competing to be the principal engine of urban planning and post-war reconstruction, were intellectually underpinned by studies such as Jane Jacobs' *The Death and Life of Great American Cities* (1961), in the work of Jan Gehl and his colleagues in Copenhagen beginning with *Life*

Between Buildings: Using Public Space (1971), and William H Whyte's *The Social Life of Small Urban Spaces* (1981). In the UK it fell to Colin, firstly in his advocacy of play in his editorship of *Anarchy* magazine, then with Anthony Fyson at the Town and Country Planning Association (TCPA) with the publication of *Streetwork*, to promote such child-centred approaches to city planning. In this they were helped by the success that followed the publication in 1959 of *The Lore and Language of Schoolchildren*, by folklorists Iona and Peter Opie, and subsequently by the couple's even more influential study, *Children's Games in Street and Playground* (1969), both books locating the street and the playground as the terrain of formative forms of sociability and common culture. In the battle between the child in the street and the car on the road, it was a foregone conclusion that the car would win. Today, 70 years later, that battle is being fought again, courtesy of Low Traffic Neighbourhoods and 'the 15 Minute City'.

Both *Streetwork* and *The Child in the City* came in tandem with the publication of the *Bulletin of Environmental Education* (BEE) by the TCPA under Fyson and Ward's editorship, which ran successfully from 1971 for two decades, inspiring teachers and local educational authorities to take urban environmental studies as a serious and necessary component of the curriculum. This led to the establishment of a number of innovative local Urban Studies Centres in London.

Equally important in the early 1970s was the Ruskin History Workshop movement, inspiring teachers to help pupils collect the reminiscences of their own parents and grand-parents – especially those from former Commonwealth countries – in the preparation of more relevant local history and social studies materials based on recording and documenting those lives and experiences. Where local or regional teachers' resource centres existed, these also began to publish teaching materials based on collecting such material. This, in the words of the Ruskin movement, was 'history from below'. Sensitivity and tact were required, however, as I realised early on when the mother of one pupil I taught sent a note back complaining, 'the less he knows about his grandfather the better as far as I am concerned, so please don't ask him again!'

Colin lived during a period when curiosity about human relations was a widening field of discussion and influence, notably in the turn to social psychology, social history and cultural studies in academia and journalism. The writings of people like Langston Hughes, C Wright Mills, Margaret Mead, Jane Jacobs, Erving Goffman, Studs Terkel, Sven Lindqvist, Mary Douglas, Richard Hoggart, Stuart Hall, Richard Titmuss, Raymond Williams and Josephine Klein – together with the work of many documentary photographers – were widely distributed and debated. The 1960s 'Penguin Revolution' in paperback publishing strongly aided this informal education process. When the weekly magazine *New Society* started in 1962, Ward was, as Sophie Scott-Brown tells us, 'an instant fan'. In fact, many of the young writers Ward had published at *Anarchy* went on to write for *New Society*, including Richard Mabey, Kate Soper and Laurie Taylor.

There is one insight of Colin's I have come to value most of all when encountering the heavy weather surrounding much political discussion. This was his warning against the assumption, particularly on the left, that the social and the political are one and the same thing and therefore interchangeable. They are not. The social is a much larger, more inclusive, more porous, more informally constructed and sustained lifeworld than the political – and therefore less easily captured by vested interests. We make and unmake the social world each day, and that is why it is so flexible and resilient. And it is why for Colin the education process was a lifelong endeavour, further enriched by being out in the world rather than sequestered within walled institutions. This is why the 'extra-mural' – literally, outside the walls – movement in adult education has always been so attractive to radical thinkers and teachers, and that lifelong learning and second-chance education have always been favoured spheres of a radical and collaborative pedagogy.

If there have to be classrooms, and there probably always will, nothing has given me more enjoyment and hope in recent years than watching Maria Speth's captivating 2021 film *Mr Bachmann and His Class*. This three-and-a-half-hour fly-on-the-wall documentary portrays the daily engagement of a teacher with a class of newly arrived children of first and second-generation immigrants, now settled near Marburg in central Germany. The classroom is revealed as a large, brightly lit atelier with large swathes of natural lighting, and enough room for rows of desks as well as a breakout area with armchairs, a day bed, a full complement of musical instruments, including keyboards, drum kit and electric guitars, plus a kitchen area with tea, coffee and snacks. The day's work moves fairly seamlessly between formal lessons and collective and individual creativity, with the teacher acting as director/choreographer. There are tears, anger and distress at times, not surprising given what some of the children and their families have gone through. Yet while such unique conditions and exceptional professional qualities cannot be universally prescribed from above, the film nevertheless provides a glimpse into how wonderful, creative and joyful the classroom can be at its best: a safe and enriching space between the home and the wider world that the children will remember, and many cherish, for the rest of their lives. The classroom and the street: it is not a case of either/or but both.

19. Reworking 'the relations between people and their environment'

Colin Ward's Quietly Radical Urbanism

Dan Hill

Our library at Melbourne School of Design contains several copies of Colin Ward's books. This well-thumbed collection indicates that the radical yet approachable ideas that Ward stood for are not at all stuck in mid-twentieth-century Britain. In fact, they seem more prescient now than at any point in the last four decades.

Like many, I first discovered Ward's work through 1978's *The Child in the City* which I used when writing 'The Dispersed School' with Catherine Burke, a chapter for *Urban Schools: Designing for High-Density* (2020). I placed his notion of 'the city as a resource' alongside that of little-known Sheffield teacher A H T Glover, who wrote *New Teaching for A New Age* (1946) and whose liberated classroom later produced the legendary industrial designer David Mellor.

I was quietly thrilled by Ward's tying-together of participative communities, bottom-up urbanism, self-organised housing and infrastructure, with everyday activities like learning and playing and art and gardening – and in the potential of distributed, decentralised cultures of organisation, decision-making, imagining and making together. Ward humbly summarised his rich body of work as 'an exploration of the relations between people and their environment'. It is that, but it is also a revelation.

Ward wrote: 'The city, before the motorcar drove them off the streets, was full of street characters, who provided the young with incidental amusement and instruction'. This idea of a street as urban theatre stuck in my mind and it was no accident that, within a couple of years, I'd be giving public talks featuring 1930s Swedish newsreels of similarly vibrant, diverse and playful streets in Stockholm. Yet as well as conveying how Stockholm streets had been a shared and diverse public space for many centuries, similarly 'full of street characters', these old films also depicted the moment that the motor car began to dominate the city's streets. Within two decades, Sweden ended up the most car-dense country in Europe and drove the diversity away from its shared public spaces, just as Ward described.

I was using these films to unlock assumptions about what streets were actually for. Working at the Swedish government's innovation agency, Vinnova, we had initiated a mission to retrofit all Swedish streets, such that they might be public spaces once again, 'healthy, sustainable and full of life'. We envisaged a loose kit of parts that could dislodge motor vehicle-dominated spaces, offering a platform for biodiverse and socially diverse places, in a way that could slowly spread across the country, led by locals. We called the project Street Moves.

The first Stockholm variants of the Street Moves kit were designed by six-year-old schoolchildren from schools on the streets we selected for the initial prototypes. We put the architects' pens in the children's hands, recognising that these people are the true experts in their street, not the transport planner at City Hall. The role of designers working on the project was to translate the children's ideas into modules, each representing desirable applications for the streetscape. These applications might be seating to encourage informal social activity, play, providing scooter and bike parking, plants, sandpits, tool sheds, chalkboards, cookers, and so on. The core design principles for Street Moves can be located precisely in Ward's *Talking to Architects*.

The kit of parts was designed and fabricated in Swedish timber, cut precisely to street edges but capable of being adapted or recycled over time. Brian Eno provided some typically inventive and generative design principles for the Street Moves pilots. Eno's principles also had a touch of wit and adventure that I hoped would counterpoint the risk aversion of transport planning. In *Freedom to Go*, Ward had noted how planners generally must 'bend to the prevailing wind, that of the highway engineers'. We have not moved on much. Whether admitted to or not, the first order object of the street remains a motor vehicle. If we give the street to traffic departments, we get traffic. Give the street to gardeners and we'd get gardens.

In Street Moves, we asked what the street might be able to create, what it might be able to do. The street becomes a place of learning. And as streets are the basic unit of cities, we are not only speculating about what streets are for, but what cities are about, what we are about.

These ideas of value tend to be intimate, idiosyncratic and everyday. When speaking of such value, Ward would often quote the early modern architect W R Lethaby, who touched on the city's 'true riches (of) learning and beauty, and music and art, coffee and omelettes'. Riches indeed.

Nordic city governments do not simply support or enable individuals. They also work to spread insights and ideas from those practices across a city equally, so that everyone benefits. While some fragile version of this sensibility was part of the British systems of planning and governance that Ward worked in and around, it has been surgically excised from the UK in recent decades. In *Talking Houses*, Ward would accurately nail the broader problem in the context of council housing, describing Britain's 'grotesque centralisation of policy', leading only to 'unwilling imposition of central policy by local councils'. The UK now has the most centralised governance in the OECD.

It also shed capability, almost rendering British councils a completely different type of entity to a municipal organisation in Helsinki, Stockholm or Oslo, say. In 1976, 49 per cent of all UK architects worked for the public sector; by 2017, the proportion working for the public sector was 0.7 per cent in England, and just 0.2 per cent in London. This has left a public sector largely without design intelligence or capability onboard.

However, needs must, and the wheel is turning, crunching through the gears. Local councils in the UK have started building actual council houses again for the first time in decades. Ward crops up in John Boughton's 2022 book, *A History of Council Housing in 100 Estates* as part of the scene that produced Walter Segal's self-build methods in Lewisham in the 1980s. I visited Segal's Walter's Way in 2017, furtively stalking the place with my camera and delighting in the various extrusions and exaptations that residents had added to their homes over the years, another influence on Street Moves.

Ward's role at Walter's Way was quiet, but significant. Ward was doing the unheralded background work of connecting Walter Segal with Brian Richardson, Assistant Borough Architect at Lewisham Council, and stimulating an informed conversation about self-organised housing. This kind of subtle coordination suggests the sensibility of the wrangler of 'dark matter' that I've become so interested in: the idea of a designer who focuses less on creating singular things, and instead looks to create the conditions from which enduring complexity can emerge.

The houses at Walter's Way endure wonderfully, continuing to be adaptable, to be valuable. Ward's words endure too. He understood that sustainability and inequality are entwined well before anyone muttered the phrase 'just transition', just as he repeatedly returned to themes that have hardly gone away: affordable housing, suburbs and regional towns, green cities and gardens, sustainable transport, locally owned renewable energies, ways of curbing land valuation, transforming education, or encouraging small enterprises with tools, technologies and training.

But Ward's advocacy for self-organised housing seems particularly relevant once again. It informs our current work in the key regional town of Shepparton, Victoria, which is facing the front line of the climate crisis with the unsustainable, largely homogenous housing that the Australian market specialises in. Inspiration is drawn directly from Ward, but also from contemporary examples which seem to embody them: Bristol's WeCanMake, which brings together community land trusts, fabrication equipment, skills development, and a participative dynamic from within the local community; the global Wikihouse movement, initiated by Alastair Parvin and Indy Johar, which aligns contemporary technologies with self-build open systems; the Accessory Dwelling Units cropping up in backyards and vacant garages in Los Angeles; the recent renaissance in European co-operative housing, particularly in cities like Zürich, Amsterdam, Bergen and Berlin, constructed without property developers and with residents working directly with architects, in highly participative design processes.

In his *Direct Action for Working Class Housing* (1984), Ward noted that, 'Everyone today is so completely dependent on housing supply systems... that we find it hard to believe that people can house themselves'. These words could have been written today here in Australia, almost four decades on, where a narrowly defined, almost completely private housing market, deliberately created by neoliberal policymaking, has hit the wall. As in the UK and USA, an entire system is out of balance, constantly veering towards new forms of damaging instability.

Yet having hit that wall, repeatedly, perhaps we might finally be seeing signs of life in alternate possible futures emerging in the examples above—in the return of quality council housing led by the likes of Camden and Enfield, working with civic-minded architects like Peter Barber, Karukusevic Carson, Mihail Riches et al, but perhaps particularly in the truly participative, open systems of WeCanMake and Wikihouse, a self-building movement powered by contemporary decentralised infrastructures.

Perhaps Ward is allowing himself a wry smile, in seeing the ideas of the early 1970s being dusted off and reimagined by a new generation, prompting this rebalancing act of local council-led invention counterpointed by self-build technologies enabling 'people to house themselves'. Having been stuck for decades, these most fundamental 'relations between people and their environment' are weaving themselves together in different ways once again, and the slim volumes containing Ward's quietly radical ideas suddenly do not feel decades-old. Rather, they increasingly feel like pattern-books for possible futures.

20. Anarchism's Good Ancestor

Roman Krznaric

It is sometimes said that Goethe was the last person in the world who knew everything. No, it was Colin Ward. By my desk I have a full shelf of his books on an extraordinary range of subjects, from allotments, rural childhood and holiday camps to urban design, the history of work and anarchist theory. Conversations with Colin could range even further – Italian opera, Brazilian politics, the Arts and Crafts movement, the novels of Tolstoy – all of it interspersed with snatches of comic songs and pithy quotes drawn from his encyclopaedic memory. Maybe Colin didn't quite know everything, but I've never met anyone with such an astonishing breadth of knowledge and curiosity about the world, coupled with a rare humility and desire to generously share all he knew.

I first met Colin and Harriet, his wonderful partner in life, in the late 1990s when I was doing a PhD in the Department of Government at the University of Essex. Colin's ideas were the perfect antidote to my studies, since he was an expert in 'non-government': in discovering the places in between, the local, the unofficial, the voices of everyday people. It is difficult to express just how much he has shaped my life, but suffice to say that I have a screensaver with favourite writers who inspire me, and right in the middle – alongside authors such as Ursula Le Guin, Sven Lindqvist and John Berger – there is Colin, peering over the top of his old typewriter. I think of him not so much judging what I write but rather offering gentle encouragement and reminding me of everything we can achieve by acting together, collectively confronting the challenges of life without resorting to the big state, big business, big anything.

In 1942, as a 16-year-old during the dark days of the Second World War, Colin copied out the following lines from an article by Bill Connor ('Cassandra') in the *Daily Mirror*: 'Our children are guarded from diphtheria by what a Japanese and a German did. They are saved from smallpox by an Englishman's work. They are saved from rabies because of a Frenchman. From birth to death they are surrounded by an invisible host – the spirits of men who never served a lesser loyalty than the welfare of mankind.'

For me, Colin is such an invisible host, whose views and ideals quietly shape my own, often without me realising it. If I look back at the books I've written over the past two decades, Colin is always there, even if he's not always directly mentioned in the index. For the last few years I've been working on a book called *History for Tomorrow*, (published in July 2024) which explores what we can learn from the past for tackling the multiple crises of the twenty-first century. In the chapter on water scarcity, I found myself writing about Valencia's *Tribunal de las Aguas* – the Tribunal of Waters – whose members are democratically elected by local farmers to manage their scarce water resources, and which has been meeting outside the West door of the city's cathedral every Thursday at noon for hundreds of years. But where had I first encountered this remarkable commons institution? In a Colin Ward book, of course – *Reflected in Water* (1997). Why is my book *Empathy* (2014) strewn with quotes from the philosopher Martin Buber? Because Colin introduced me to his work via his own book *Influences: Voices of Creative Dissent* (1991). Why does another of my books, *Carpe Diem Regained* (2017), describe Peter Kropotkin's daring escape from prison? You guessed it: Colin again.

Perhaps at a deeper level, my ideas have been fundamentally shaped by Colin's relational perspective on the world. He loved to quote the German anarchist Gustav Landauer, who wrote: 'The state is not something which can be destroyed by a revolution, but is a condition, a certain relationship between human beings, a mode of human behaviour; we destroy it by contracting other relationships, by behaving differently.'

All my own writing, at its core, is about trying to understand relationships – not just conceiving the state as a relational entity rather than as a structure or some kind of machine, but also attempting to explore the filigree of human relationships that underpin all our economic organisations and social institutions, as well as our relationship with future generations and the planet we live on. We are relational beings born into interdependence with each other and with the living world on which all life depends. If we forget this, if we remain encapsulated in an atomistic individualism, civilisational tragedy awaits.

For all of the intellectual inspiration I have imbibed from Colin, he has influenced my life as much off the page as on it. Would I have built my kitchen with my own hands if it weren't for Colin introducing me to Walter Segal and the self-build housing movement? Would I have an allotment today if it weren't for reading the book he co-authored with David Crouch, The *Allotment: It's Landscape and Culture* (1988)? Would I have spent so much time exploring the plotland settlements of Jaywick on the Essex coast if not for Colin, who brought it all to life in his pioneering book with Dennis Hardy, *Arcadia for All: The Legacy of a Makeshift Landscape* (1984)?

Colin would probably be a little perturbed to discover that his impact on me, or anybody, had been so great. That was all part of his modesty. But I think it is a true reflection of the path I have taken. That's not to say that I think Colin's work is the key to all mythologies. There is plenty I doubt or disagree with. I can't see how we can rein in the giant fossil fuel corporations without using the regulatory power of the state: all the local community solar initiatives in the world won't free us from their destructive influence. The same goes for the Big Tech firms that are plundering our personal data for sale to the highest bidder and who dominate emerging fields such as artificial intelligence and genetic engineering. And can Colin's brand of everyday anarchism, rooted in local, voluntary organisations, really confront the colossal wealth inequalities between the Global North and South, or institutionalised racism that gets passed on from generation to generation, or the turbulence that might result from a billion migrants being on the move by 2050?

At the same time, Colin's work is a reminder that there are no simple blueprints for tackling such issues. We are unlikely to find the answers in either benign dictators or benign bureaucracies. We will need to experiment, to improvise, to discover surprising solutions in unexpected places. And that's all so very Wardian. I also believe that our greatest hope for meeting the challenges of the global ecological crisis is going to be through innovations at the city level, such as cities based on radical circular production or the principles of doughnut economics. We may see the emergence of something like bioregional city-states over coming decades, and Colin's writings are likely to become an essential resource, taking us back to the work of Kropotkin and Ebenezer Howard, and to Colin's own insights into forging mutual aid in the cities of tomorrow.

Colin's writings – indeed his whole life – also encourage us to favour practice over theory, to ground who we are and what we do in the realities of lived experience. One of my favourite stories about him – which I may have unconsciously embellished over the years – concerns his period as a teacher of the new-fangled subject of Liberal Studies at Wandsworth Technical College in South London during the 1960s. Most of his students were young apprentices in the building trade, and when he walked in to teach his first class he asked them what it was they wanted to learn – what difficulties did they face in their lives that he could really help them with? It turned out that their greatest concern was with lack of sleep. So Colin duly crammed his brain full of research on sleep and set about teaching a term of classes on the art of sleeping. It is a story that has always stayed with me as a teacher, the ultimate example of making an effort to meet your students' needs. But it also speaks, in a wider sense, to the importance of meeting reality head on rather than taking flights of fancy into utopianism. Yes, we can dream of an ideal future, but let's not allow that to distract us from the fierce urgency of the now.

The immunologist Jonas Salk – who developed the first polio vaccine in the 1950s – said that the great question facing humanity is this: 'Are we being good ancestors?' In other words, how will we be remembered by the generations to come for what we did or didn't do when we had the chance?

Colin Ward, you will be remembered as a good ancestor. Of that I have no doubt.

The Contributors

Catherine Burke is Emerita Professor of the History of Education at the University of Cambridge. Before moving into higher education, she worked as a tutor for the Sheffield Adult Education Service, the Workers' Education Association and the Northern College. Her publications include *Education, Childhood and Anarchism: Talking Colin Ward* (2014), edited with Ken Jones.

Luca Csepely-Knorr is research chair in architecture at the University of Liverpool School of Architecture. Her research focuses on the histories of architecture, landscape architecture and urban design from the late nineteenth century to the 1970s.

Tessa Coombes was a Labour councillor in Bristol for eight years (1994-2002). She also worked at Hartcliffe Community Campus; UWE Bristol; was chief executive of the Western Partnership for Sustainable Development and spent eight years at Business West as director of policy and strategy.

Rob Cowan is editor of *Context* (the journal of the Institute of Historic Building Conservation), author of *The Dictionary of Urbanism* and a cartoonist.

Gillian Darley is a widely published writer, biographer and broadcaster. She co-authored *Tomorrow's New Communities*

(Joseph Rowntree Foundation, 1991) with David Lock and Peter Hall. *Villages of Vision* was republished by Five Leaves Publications in 2007. Her most recent book is *Excellent Essex* (Old Street Publishing, 2019). She was awarded an OBE in 2015 'for services to the built environment and its conservation'.

Paul Dobraszczyk is an architectural writer and lecturer at the Bartlett School of Architecture, London. He is the author of many books, the most recent being *Animal Architecture: Beasts, Buildings and Us* (Reaktion, 2023) and *Architecture and Anarchism: Building Without Authority* (Paul Holberton, 2021).

Alice Ferguson is a co-founder of the Playing Out movement. She and her neighbour, Amy Rose, developed the temporary play street model on their own road in 2009. Playing Out CIC grew out of that idea and action, responding to interest from other parents, residents, experts and organisations. She continued to co-lead the organisation until 2023. Now, as an associate of Playing Out, she focuses on projects, development, strategy, advocacy, campaigning, public speaking and writing work towards the long-term vision of Playing Out, to restore children's freedom.

Ted Fowler started working life in farming and fishing. Since moving to Bristol, he has developed transport, education, inclusion and finance initiatives. He remains involved in many community activities.

Dan Hill is Director of the Melbourne School of Design, and a Professor of the Built Environment at the University of Melbourne. He is a designer, urbanist, and educator, working at the intersection of design, technology and cities. He held the position of Director of Strategic Design for the Swedish Government's innovation agency, Vinnova, from 2019 to 2022, and has also worked at Arup, SITRA (the Finnish public innovation fund), and the BBC.

Andrew Kelly was director of Bristol Ideas 1993-2024. He was director of Festival of Ideas for 17 years and Festival of the Future City for 10 years. He is the author of many books on film history, the future of cities, Isambard Kingdom Brunel, and Bristol.

Ruth Kinna is Professor of Political Theory at Loughborough University. She is a political theorist and historian of ideas with research interests in anarchism, nineteenth and early twentieth century socialist thought, utopianism and contemporary radicalism. She is co-editor of the journal Anarchist Studies.

David Knight is a designer, strategist and author, and founding co-director, with Cristina Monteiro of the architecture, planning and research practice DK-CM. Together David and Cristina edited *Public House: A cultural and social history of the London pub* (Open City, 2021).

Roman Krznaric is a public philosopher who writes about the power of ideas to change society. His latest book is *History for*

Tomorrow: Inspiration from the Past for the Future of Humanity. His previous books have been published in more than 25 languages. He is senior research fellow at Oxford University's Centre for Eudaimonia and Human Flourishing and founder of the world's first Empathy Museum.

Martin Parker works at the University of Bristol Business School. His recent books are *Shut Down the Business School* (Pluto, 2018), *Anarchism, Organization and Management* (Routledge, 2020) and *Life After COVID19* (Bristol University Press, 2020).

Sol Pérez-Martínez is an architect, educator and a postdoctoral research fellow at ETH Zürich in the European Research Council project 'Women Writing Architecture 1700-1900'. Before her academic positions, she ran an architectural practice in Chile where she and her firm partners developed a public school that inspired her research about architecture, education and politics. She was awarded a doctorate by UCL in 2022 for 'Learn where you stand: Lessons for civic engagement in architecture and the built environment from the Urban Studies Centres Network and their situated pedagogies in Britain 1968–1988'.

Dr Amber Roberts is Lecturer in Urban Design at the University of Manchester. Her research focuses on questions of spatial justice, class and cultural identity in historic and contemporary landscapes.

Sheila Rowbotham, who helped start the women's liberation movement in Britain, is known internationally as an historian of feminism and radical social movements. She is the author of *Women, Resistance and Revolution* (1972); *Woman's Consciousness, Man's World* (1973); *Hidden from History* (1973) and other titles.

Sophie Scott-Brown is programme director for the Europaeum (Oxford). Her research focuses on radical democracy and activism. She is the author of *The Histories of Raphael Samuel* (2017) and *Colin Ward and the Art of Anarchy* (2022).

Martin Stott has retired from a career in environment and sustainability in local government. He is chair of Writers in Oxford and a former chair of the William Morris Society. He moonlights as a photographer and blogs as 'Lord Muck' about growing, cooking, composting and other earthy matters.

Stuart White is a lecturer in the Department of Politics and International Relations, Oxford University and fellow in politics, Jesus College, Oxford. He is interested in egalitarianism, its application in institutions, and in currents of thinking both anti-capitalist and anti-authoritarian.

Ken Worpole is a writer and social historian and has published books on architecture, landscape and public policy. His most recent book is *No Matter How Many Skies Have Fallen: Back to the Land in Wartime Britain* (2021). According to the *New*

Statesman, 'Worpole is a literary original, a social and architectural historian whose books combine the Orwellian ideal of common decency with understated erudition.'

Patrick Wright is Emeritus Professor of Literature, History and Politics, King's College, London and for many years before this a self-employed writer, broadcaster and journalist. His latest book is *The Sea View Has Me Again: Uwe Johnson in Sheerness* (December 2020).

Acknowledgments

I owe thanks to many people who have helped with *Mutual Aid, Everyday Anarchy*. Work started three years ago when a small group started to discuss projects which might take place in 2024 for the Colin Ward centenary. That group grew larger, and more ideas were put forward. The end of Bristol Ideas in April 2024 meant that our work on this ended though some projects will be taken forward by those involved. I am grateful to the board of Bristol Ideas for their support over the years and for providing a grant as part of the legacy programme for this book. My colleague Amy O'Beirne did much of the early work and Melanie Kelly helped with editorial matters.

I am grateful to the authors of each essay for their work and patience as this book took longer to appear than thought originally. Special thanks are due to Ken Worpole and Roman Krznaric who provided advice and help over the years. And thanks too to Ross Bradshaw – one of those who helps keep the Ward flame burning – for publishing this book. Everyone involved has helped to ensure that not only is Colin Ward – a modest man who influenced many people – not forgotten, but that his ideas live on.

Andrew Kelly
August, 2024

Further Reading

By Colin Ward (unless stated)

The Allotment: Its Landscape and Culture, with David Crouch (Faber, 1977), (Five Leaves, 1997), (Little Toller, 2023)

Anarchism: People and Ideas, with an introduction by Ruth Kinna (Five Leaves 2024) – an updated version of *Anarchism: a very short introduction* (OUP, 2004)

Anarchy In Action (Allen & Unwin, 1973 and various subsequent editions by Freedom Press)

Arcadia For All, with Dennis Hardy (Mansell, 1984), Five Leaves, 2004)

Art and the Built Environment, with Eileen Adams (Longman, 1982)

Autonomy, Solidarity, Possibility – A Colin Ward Reader, edited by Chris Wilbert and Damien F. White (AK Press, 2011)

Chartres: The Making of a Miracle (Folio Society, 1986)

The Child in the City (Architectural Press, 1978), (Bedford Square Press, 1990), with photographs by Ann Golzen and others

The Child in the Country (Robert Hale, 1988), (Bedford Square Press, 1990)

Cotters and Squatters (Five Leaves, 2002)

The Factory We Never Had, with A Factory As It Might Be, by William Morris, pamphlet (Old Hammond Press, 1984)

Freedom To Go: After the Motor Age (Freedom Press, 1991)

Goodnight Campers! History of the British Holiday Camp, with Dennis Hardy (Mansell, 1986), Five Leaves (2010)

Havens and Springboards: The Foyer Movement in Context (Calouste Gulbenkian, 1997)

Housing: An Anarchist Approach (Freedom Press, 1976)

Housing is Freedom, Housing is Theft, pamphlet (Old Hammond Press, 1984)

Images of Childhood in Old Photographs, with Tim Ward (Sutton, 1991)

Influences: Voices of Creative Dissent (Green Books, 1991)

New Town, Home Town: The Lessons of Experience (Calouste Gulbenkian, 1993)

Reflected in Water: A Crisis of Social Responsibility (Cassell, 1987)

Sociable Cities, with Peter Hall (Academic Press, 1999)

Social Policy: An Anarchist Response (LSE, 1996), (Freedom Press 2000)

Streetwork: The Exploding School, with Tony Fyson (Routledge, 1973)

Talking Anarchy, with David Goodway (Five Leaves 2003)

Talking to Architects (Freedom Press, 1996)

Talking Green (Five Leaves, 2012)

Talking Houses (Freedom Press, 1990)

Talking Schools (Freedom Press, 1995)

Tenants Take Over (Architectural Press, 1974)

Undermining the Central Line, with Ruth Rendell (Chatto, 1989)

Utopia (Penguin, 1974)

Violence – Connexions (Penguin Connexions, 1970)

Welcome Thinner Cities (NCVO, 1989)

When We Build Again, Let's Have Housing That Works (Pluto Press, 1987)

Work (Penguin Connexions, 1972)

Edited by Colin Ward

British School Buildings: Designs and Appraisals (Architectural Press, 1976)

Fields, Factories and Workshops, by Peter Kropotkin (Allen and Unwin, 1974 and other editions)

Memoirs of a Revolutionist (Folio Society, 1978 and other editions)

Vandalism (Architectural Press, 1973)

Related publications

Anarchist Seeds Beneath the Snow: Left-Libertarian Thought and British Writers from William Morris to Colin Ward, by David Goodway (Liverpool Univ Press, 2006)

Autonomy: The Cover Designs of Anarchy 1961-1970, edited by Dan Poyner (Hyphen, 2012)

A Beautiful Idea: History of the Freedom Press Anarchists, by Rob Ray (Freedom Press, 2018)

Colin Ward and the Art of Everyday Anarchy, by Sophie Scott-Brown (Routledge, 2022)

A British Anarchist Tradition: Herbert Read, Alex Comfort and Colin Ward, by Carissa Honeywell (Bloomsbury, 2011)

Colin Ward: Life, Times and Thought, edited by Carl Levy (Lawrence and Wishart, 2014)

A Decade of Anarchy 1961-1970, edited by Damian F. White and Chris Wilbert (Freedom Press, 1987)

*Education, Childhood and Anarchism: Talking Colin W*ard, edited by Catherine Burke and Ken Jones (Routledge, 2016)

Freedom: A Hundred Years, October 1886-October 1986, edited by Donald Rooum and others

A Man of Small Importance: My Father Griffin Barry, by Harriet Ward (Dormouse Books, 2003)

Remembering Colin Ward 1924-2010, edited by Ross Bradshaw, Harriet Ward and Ken Worpole (Five Leaves, 2011)

Richer Futures: Fashioning a New Future, edited by Ken Worpole (Earthscan, 1999

Stamps: Designs for Anarchist Postage Stamps, illustrated by Clifford Harper (Rebel Press, 1997)

Freedom, War Commentary, Anarchy, The Raven, www.thesparrowsnest.org.uk

Anarchist Studies, Especially Issue 19, *The Colin Ward Issue* edited by Ruth Kinna (Lawrence & Wishart, 2011)

Note – some titles are available in North American editions and later editions from other publishers and some titles are available in translation